THE WARZECHAS OF MUSTANG MOTT

STORIES OF THE LIVES AND LOVED ONES OF VINCENT WILLIAM AND SUSIE DRZYMALA WARZECHA

ANTHONY WARZECHA

Order this book online at www.trafford.com
or email orders@trafford.com

Most Trafford titles are also available at major online book retailers.

Printed in the United States of America.

ISBN: 978-1-4669-2176-4 (sc)
ISBN: 978-1-4669-2177-1 (hc)
ISBN: 978-1-4669-2175-7 (e)

Library of Congress Control Number: 2012905588

Trafford rev. 03/23/2012

 www.trafford.com

North America & international
toll-free: 1 888 232 4444 (USA & Canada)
phone: 250 383 6864 ♦ fax: 812 355 4082

CONTENTS

Mom and Dad,

We love you!

Our prayer always is:

"May your souls and the souls of all the faithful departed, through the mercy of God, rest in peace. Amen."

PREFACE

This anthology of recollections and stories of the lives and loved ones of Vincent and Susie Warzecha is an expression of the love and devotion of this couple and their family for each other.

The work originated as a project to occupy the time of a retiree who might otherwise slip into a wasteland of uselessness, boredom, and, worst of all, aggravation to his spouse. It certainly accomplished its purpose, and then some. As it progressed from a few pages of remembrances by family members of life in the home of Vincent and Susie (Dad and Mom to some of us and Grandpa and Grandma to others) to the volume in your hands at the moment, the author found himself absorbed almost to the point of addiction with the research needed to produce this book.

I must admit that, at times, the challenge seemed greater than the endurance and ability of yours truly, but faith in the nobility of the project and the need for its completion were powerful forces. It is my hope that each reader will find himself or herself drawn more closely into the circle of affection reflected by the many complex members of this family.

In an effort to reduce the confusion created by the various terms by which the central characters are addressed, let it be known that I will sometimes refer to Mom and Dad (Grandma and Grandpa to some of you and Great-Grandma and Great-Grandpa to others and something else to the rest of you) as Mom and Dad sometimes and as Susie and Vincent at other times. It will always be clear to me to whom I am referring and I hope you can keep up with me.

Relax now and enjoy a story that may be too good to be true, but which is believed by each participant. We have meant to be truthful at all times except when we identify a story as pure fantasy or wishful thinking. When we resort to speculation or conjecture, it is based on the best evidence we could find at the time. One important point we can rely on is that the truthfulness of each story is as good as the storytellers' memories.

CHAPTER ONE

THE BEGINNING

THE WARZECHA/DRZYMALA UNION

"Do you, Vincent, take Susie for your lawfully wedded wife, to have and to hold from this day forward in sickness and in health, for better or for worse, until death do you part?", asked Father Peter Grzcsiak, pastor of Holy Cross Catholic Church in Yorktown. He spoke in Polish which was the language of the parish and the people gathered in the church. "I do", responded Vincent in a positive but gentle voice. "And do you, Susie, take Vincent for your lawfully wedded husband, to have and to hold from this day forward in sickness and in health, for better or for worse, until death do you part?" intoned the priest. In a soft clear voice and with eyes shining with joy and admiration for her husband-to-be, the bride answered, "I do."

As the ceremony proceeded on that hot August morning with the church windows open and the fans blowing to provide ventilation, perspiration beaded on their foreheads and those of Pete Warzecha, brother of the groom and his best man and Anna Warzecha, cousin of the groom and the maid of honor.

"With this ring, I thee wed . . .", the couple repeated in Polish, pledging their lives to be joined into one for their common good and the salvation of their souls and for whatever children God would give them.

The ceremony ended with the priest, in the name of the triune God, blessing them in the Sacrament of Matrimony. They were the happiest people on earth.

While we don't know for sure exactly what went through everyone's minds, we can feel reasonably certain thoughts similar to these popped into their heads as the couple walked arm in arm down the aisle as Mr. and Mrs. Vincent Warzecha:

Vincent: "She sure is beautiful. I'm lucky to have won her heart. Now, don't trip on your own feet or hers and be sure to smile at everyone."

Susie: "Now what?"

Bride's mother: "She's only nineteen. What does she know about being a wife and who's going to help me with all the housework now. Irene's only ten."

Bride's father: "Vincent is a good man, from a fine family. He will be an excellent husband."

Maid-of-honor: "Vincent is so handsome. If we weren't cousins, maybe . . . Oh well."

Best man: "Wonder when my turn will come."

Groom's mother: "All the sons are married now except Ben and Pete. Susie will be a fine wife for him. She comes from a big family and sure knows how to care for little ones."

Groom's father: "My helpers are just about all gone from home now. A man and a woman start out all by themselves and that's the way they end up. Pretty soon it'll be just Katie and me."

Father Grzcsiak: "They are a fine couple. She is from a family with eight children and he's from one with seven. May God bless them and give them an abundance of children and a good life together."

It was Tuesday morning, August 26, 1924 in Yorktown, Texas. The ceremony had begun at ten o'clock with the sun shining brightly even though there were hints of rain. The area was in the midst of a dry spell bordering on drought conditions. On Monday, the temperature was 78 degrees at 7 AM, but it hit 103 before the day was over. It was perfect weather for harvesting cotton. In fact, the weekly Yorktown News reported in its August 28 edition that 3,035 bales of cotton had been ginned by the five gins in town with the average price for middling grade ranging between 24 and 25 cents a pound. It was also reported through August 30, 1923 the local area produced 2,194 bales compared to 3,920 for the same period in 1922. There were mixed feelings with the arrival of showers Tuesday night which broke the dry spell. Slightly cooler temperatures prevailed that night after the rain.

Relatives had come from Falls City, San Antonio, Kosciusco, Panna Maria, Cuero and the area around Yorktown. They had traveled by automobiles and horse drawn buggies. Some folks thought Vincent and Susie could have chosen a cooler time of the year to get married, but who knows what goes through young peoples' minds when they plan their lives. Maybe the abundant cotton crop in the fields had some effect on their decision to wed at that time. Maybe each participant did not want to delay the event lest the other would back out or find someone else. Who knows? In any event, they had chosen the time to begin their lives together and there was no turning back.

Vincent Warzecha was the sixth of seven sons of August and Katie Kaminski Warzecha of the Lindenau community near Cuero in DeWitt County. Susie was the eldest daughter and the second oldest offspring of Steve Adam and Bena Josephine Snoga Drzymala of Yorktown.

On the occasion of their golden wedding anniversary in 1974, they reminisced with the following account of their courtship:

"Fifty-two years ago, a tall good-looking young man met a shy, beautiful young lady at a house dance at Bock's Place near Yorktown. They saw each other from time to time at dances and at friends' homes until courtship set in. He had to travel from where he lived in the Mustang Mott community to Yorktown where she lived. Susie Drzymala was a good catch and Vincent knew it. He wore out two horses and one buggy on that dusty road to Yorktown. When he was about out of horses and she was receiving invitations from all those Yorktown boys, Vincent decided to take drastic action. He bought a Ford Model T Roadster and went calling. Susie decided that anyone with that much determination had to be the best choice she could make."

It was fitting that this young couple would bring themselves together into a new life in Holy Cross Church. They had each received their educations in Catholic schools where they had developed strong feelings for following the will of God. In forming one life together from two separate beings, they dedicated their lives to fulfilling the purpose for which God had made them.

There would be good times as well as hard times, but never did their faith in God or their belief that He would provide for their needs falter or waver. They saw to it that their children lived the Catholic faith as they understood the teachings of the Church. Their lives and the good that they imparted are testimony to how God rewards those who acknowledge their roles in His plan.

With the marriage ceremony concluded, the couple greeted the witnesses and guests in front of church before proceeding to her folks' home for the reception. A feast had been prepared by the families and friends who gathered for the occasion.

The Drzymala home was at the corner of Third Street and Church Street and was a magnificent structure befitting the family of a businessman of Steve Drzymala's stature. The yard was large and well groomed with summer flowers in beds near the base of the house. Susie's brothers had prepared the yard for the celebration, setting up tables and chairs in appropriate groupings so the guests could enjoy the outdoor atmosphere. Inside the house, the ladies had arranged seating for the matrons and the young mothers who cared for the small children. The parent's bedroom had been set aside for the infants and smallest children. Susie's sister Helen was only nine months old and just learning to walk. Other infants about the same age were Vincent's brother Frank's daughter Eleanor and his brother Joe's daughter Lillian. Youngsters of all ages roamed the house and grounds enjoying the celebration.

Behind the house and facing Third Street was the two story red tile building which housed the Yorktown Bottling and Ice Cream Works. The coolness of the lower floor was where Susie's brother Henry set up the cask of homemade mustang grape wine that Vincent's father brought for the men. Even though prohibition was in effect by virtue of the National Prohibition Act, which had been ratified as the 18th Amendment to the U.S. Constitution, it was legal to make alcoholic beverages for one's own use in his own home. A simple point was being stretched a little here, but as long as no attention was directed toward or complaints received about the activity, it was perfectly acceptable to toast the bride and groom and wish them much happiness. In fact, to not do so would certainly attract attention even if it didn't develop any complaints.

The young couple had to spend the entire day and then some under the watchful eyes of family and friends. Try as they might they could not slip out of sight of someone else even for one moment. Any display of affection for each other or of joy of the occasion had to be done in view of their well-wishers. Much laughter and merriment was evident. No one could question the fact that the Drzymalas had put on a fine feast for their first daughter's wedding.

As the day wore on, the Drzymala menfolk brought out their musical instruments and entertained the party with lively renditions of all the popular songs of the time. The front porch provided the stage as it faced the east and the setting sun in the west created a shaded front yard for the guests.

On the preceeding Saturday morning, Vincent and Susie appeared before Mr. J. T. Newman, County Clerk of DeWitt County, and fulfilled the requirements for a Marriage License. The license was issued and signed by Mrs. Emil Freund, Deputy County Clerk. The original copy of this license was located by the author during research for this history in the County Clerk's archives. It remains in my custody. It bears the certification of Reverend P. Grzcsiak that he united this couple in marriage on the 26th day of August, 1924. This civil certificate was subsequently recorded in Volume P, Page 372 of the Marriage License Record of DeWitt County on the 16th day of September, 1924.

It is interesting to note that Father Grzcsiak was Pastor of St. Anne's Church in Koscuisko from 1912 to 1915 when Susie was a little girl and her family attended church there. He had come to the United States on September 3, 1907 aboard the vessel President Lincoln which sailed from Hamburg, Germany, according to his Declaration of Intention filed with the Middle District of Pennsylvania on the 26th day of May, 1909. This document describes Father Grzesiak (spelling differs on various documents as was common in those days) as being five feet four inches tall, weighing

156 pounds, having fair complexion, brown hair, gray eyes and no visible distinctive marks. He was born in Czerinchow, Galicia, Austria on the 25th day of June, 1881. He filed a Petition For Naturalization with the District Court of Wilson County, Texas on October 14, 1914. The court ordered Father Grzesiak to be granted Citizenship on May 15, 1915. His obituary published in The Southern Messenger of San Antonio, Texas identified his place of birth as Cracow, Poland in April 1881 and his death in Yorktown, Texas on March 16, 1932 while he was Pastor of Holy Cross Church and Dean of the local deanery. The death certificate recorded in Volume Four, Page 227 of the Death Record of DeWitt County reflects the cause of death to have been Angina Pectoris (Sudden) and time of death as 5:45 AM on March 16, 1932. L. W. Nowierski, M.D. was the certifying physcian. Father Grzesiak was very much a part of Vincent and Susie's life and a favorite priest of theirs.

Mom and Dad said their wedding celebration went on for two days as was the custom with the Polish people. For one thing, some people had come from great distances (for the 1920s) and there was much visiting to do. The only occasions for get-togethers were weddings and funerals and the most was made of those events. All the news on all the family members was passed on and round to everyone and it was done in the spirit of catching up on family history and events rather than in the spirit of gossiping. Mom and Dad also told us about the custom of the day of having a charivari (pronounced and sometimes spelled shivaree) defined as a noisy mock serenade to newly weds. It seems that their friends and relatives made every effort possible to prevent the newlyweds from having any privacy for the first few days of marriage. Perhaps, this is what gave rise to the newly weds developing the custom of a fast get away after the reception for a honeymoon in some secret location. At any rate, this young couple certainly had a festive beginning of their marriage.

The following news item appeared on the front page of the August 28, 1924 edition of the weekly Yorktown News:

MARRIED

The marriage of Miss Susie Drzymala, a popular young lady of this city, and Vincent Warzecha, a prominent young farmer of the Lindenau section was solemnized Tuesday morning at the Catholic Church, Rev. P. Grzesiak officiating.

After the ceremony the bridal party and guests were escorted to the home of the bride's parents, Mr. and Mrs. S. A. Drzymala, where a sumptuous dinner and supper were served.

The bride is the oldest daughter of S. A. Drzymala, proprietor of the Yorktown Bottling and Ice Cream Works and is well and favorably known in Yorktown and vicinity. The groom is the son of Mr. and Mrs. August Warzecha, substantial citizens of Lindenau. They will reside on the groom's farm near Lindenau.

The News joins a host of friends in extending wishes for a prosperous and happy married life.

And so, it all began: THE WARZECHAS OF MUSTANG MOTT

To this couple were born seven children. They were:

Name	Date of Birth	Married to
Rose Marie	09-08-1925	Anton F. Tam Jr.
Vincent Joseph	07-08-1927	Barbara Striedel
Ladislaus William	01-23-1929	Elinor Ryan
Anthony Benedict	03-21-1931	Dawn Wright
Newton Michael	10-30-1934	Mary Carruthers/Suzi Smith
Robert Lee	09-12-1937	Beverly Fanty
David August	09-12-1941	Marian Speed/Patsy Seidel

CHAPTER TWO

BEFORE THE BEGINNING

THE POLISH PEOPLE

The Polish nation evolved during the ninth and tenth centuries from Slavic tribes in Eastern Europe, a result primarily of the people's desire to be free from domination by other people. During these formative years, Christianity came to the area and the people's embracement of this religion became the bond that held them together.

Early history of the Polish Empire reflects periods of expansion and decline, peace and turbulence, prosperity and poverty, strength and weakness. Even into modern times, that is, the twenty-first century, Poland has been a pawn used by its neighbors to satisfy their own greedy expansion goals. The Polish people never started a fight, but they never backed away from defending themselves, either.

During the mid-1800s, the Polish people were subject to the Russian, Austrian and Prussian Empires. Even though these people often found themselves dominated by neighboring regimes, they maintained their distinctive character, customs, language, and Catholic religion. In 1831, the Poles declared their independence from foreign domination, but their rebellion was crushed. As a result, repressive sanctions were imposed on the people, heightening the atmosphere for escape.

It was in this climate that a young Catholic priest named Leopold Bonaventura Moczygemba played the most significant role in the migration of Polish settlers to America, and specifically to Texas. During his early teens, he joined the religious order of Friars Minor Conventual and was sent to Italy for his studies. After receiving an age dispensation so he could be ordained early, he became a priest in 1847 at the age of twenty-two. He was sent to Germany for further studies as he pursued his desire to be a missionary in some distant part of the world, apparently without any specific locality in mind, only where the Holy Spirit would lead him. Fate or Providence cast Father Moczygemba into the eye of Bishop Jean-Marie Odin, Bishop of Galveston, Texas who was travelling in Europe in 1852 seeking financial support for his diocese in the growing land of many freedoms but little money, many opportunities but little resources, many hardships but little oppression. The young priest wasted no time in submitting his request for assignment to this foreign land. With his superior's blessings, he and three other friars travelled to Texas, arriving in Galveston in September 1852. Father Moczygemba was assigned to the New Braunfels parish which ministered to the German settlers in the area. In 1854, he was assigned to the Alsatian colony at Castroville.

Partly because he was homesick for his countrymen and partly because he wanted to help them, he wrote glowing letters to his family and friends in Upper Silesia, the area from which he originated. He had grown up in a small village between the towns of Strzelce and Toszek, which is roughly half way between the current cities of Opole and Katowice. His letters told of the open country free of restrictive oppression and government intervention, a land where people were free to pursue their livelihood as they saw fit, a land where people could own their own land and businesses, a land where they could worship God in the

Catholic tradition, a land where all young men did not have to submit to military service of their despised rulers, and on and on, he went. He had observed the successes that the German people who he ministered to were enjoying and saw the land opportunities available. He urged the people to sell their belongings except what they could bring and what they would need in this new land.

His letters were, without a doubt, passed around the communities and parishes where they were discussed at great length. Economic conditions in Upper Silesia were tragic. Recent agrarian reforms had reduced the property holdings and therefore the ability to earn a living. The reforms had drastic effects on the peasants.

Family members huddled together to discuss and debate what to do. There really were no easy answers. The questions were difficult but simple.

What do we do?

Should we stay in Poland which is our home?

For years and years, for generations and generations our families have survived. And, yes, many have perished. Our cemeteries are full of those who could not handle the hardships.

But, this is our home.

Yes, but what kind of home do we have now and is this what we want our children to face all their lives?

Suppose we go to America.

Father Moczygemba has been there and he says we can have a better life there.

Anything is better than what we have here.

What about the hardships we will face, the long journey, all the uncertainities, a new language, a new way of living?

What shall we do?

There was so much they had to think about.

In the end, those who decided to go to the new land were the bravest, the strongest, the most optimistic, or maybe, the most desperate. At any rate, what separated those who left the old home for a new one from those who stayed was the ability to let the advantages override the disadvantages.

There is a Historic Marker which was erected in 1966 at Panna Maria, Texas which gives this account of the Polish settlement:

"Settled by 100 Polish families who came to Texas to gain economic, political and religious freedom.

Led by Father Leopold Moczygemba, O.F.M. Conv., they made a contract in 1854 with John Twohig, a San Antonio banker and merchant for land at this site.

The colonists, natives of Upper Silesia and Krakow, landed at Galveston after a hard voyage of nine weeks on a sailing ship. They hired Mexican carts to haul their farm implements, feather beds, and the cross from their parish church in Poland. The 800 men, women and children walked, some in boots, others barefoot, the 200 miles to their new home. Babies were born on the way and some of the people died. All suffered from hunger and exposure.

On December 24, 1854, they reached this site. They named it Panna Maria (Virgin Mary) placing it under the patronage of the Immaculate Conception. Beneath a large oak tree, they offered their first Midnight Mass of Thanksgiving and petition for strength and courage.

They camped out until they could put up huts of mud, straw, or wood, later building in stone. In spite of hardships, they founded a stable community, aided in settling other frontiers, pioneered in education and gave Texas many patriotic dedicated citizens."

Other groups followed these early pioneers and found life in this new land both wonderful and miserable, both what they expected and what they could not imagine in their wildest dreams.

And so, in their own ways and at their own time, four families sold all their possessions except what they needed and could transport to the new land. At separate times and in separate groups, these four families boarded trains for the shipyards from which they would leave Europe and headed to America, the great land of promise and opportunity. None of these settlers ever returned to their native home.

These four families were the WARZECHA, KAMINSKI, DRZYMALA, AND SNOGA families, all unknown to each other but determined to forge a better life for themselves.

It was from these for families that our principals, VINCENT WARZECHA and SUSIE DRZYMALA, would come forth.

THE WARZECHA FAMILY

The Warzecha family from which our subject, Vincent, originated descended from Jan (Johann) (John) and Malgorzata (Margaret) Kuczka Warzecha.

Jan was born January 23, 1826 in Poland and died June 18, 1869 in Yorktown, Texas. He married Malgorzata Kuczka in 1849. She was born July 13, 1824 in Poland and died November 4, 1910 in Yorktown, Texas. They were both buried in the Holy Cross Catholic Cemetery in Yorktown.

They left their home in Poland in early October 1855 with their two children, Joseph (aged 5) and Julius (aged 2). The trip was extremely difficult and young Julius died aboard ship and was buried at sea. This was particularly hard on the young mother who was pregnant with their third child.

They eventually arrived at the seaport at Indianola, Texas in late December 1855 and proceeded by foot with the other Polish settlers to Panna Maria, 200 miles inland, where Father Moczygemba had established a community of Polish immigrants. They later moved to Yorktown in DeWitt County.

DeWitt County Court Record, Volume E, Page 139 reflects Jan Warzecha's declaration on March 8, 1862 to become a citizen of the Confederate States of America. The same Court Record shows that on September 25, 1865, he filed for and received citizenship in the United States of America.

Confederate Army records show he served in the 6th Texas Infantry Regiment, Company I as a 2nd Sergeant under the command of Captain C. P. Naunheim.

DeWitt County Deed Records (Volume J, Pages 236 and 237) show that Jan Warzecha purchased 30 acres of land one and one half miles northeast of Yorktown for $90.00. The deed was dated August 9, 1862. On April 13, 1866, he purchased 76 acres next to that 30 acres as shown in Volume K, Pages 193-194. On April 28, 1866, he purchased 17.5 acres adjacent to the other property (see Volume K, Pages 369-370). On December 5, 1868, he deeded the 17.5 acres to his wife Margaret (Malgorzata) as her separate and personal property with the comment: "for and in consideration of the love and affection which I have for my beloved wife Margaret Warzecha and for the further consideration of my having used her separate funds." Interesting, huh!!

To this union were born six children. They were:

Joseph	born 09-18-1850 in Poland,	died 10-17-1933
Julius	born 1853 in Poland	died 11-??-1855
Konstantine	born 05-20-1856 in Panna Maria	08-26-1913
August	born 08-18-1859 in Panna Maria	12-05-1942
Maria	born 07-18-1862 in Panna Maria	02-04-1933
Stanick	born 02-26-1868 in Yorktown	02-02-1930

Our subject, Vincent, is a son of August. We will visit him later.

THE KAMINSKI FAMILY

Thomas Kaminski and his wife Catherine (Katrina) Lukaswitz Kaminski immigrated to Texas from Prussian held Poland in 1870 and they settled in Yorktown.

On May 17, 1892, Thomas filed a Declaration of Intention to become a citizen of the United States as is recorded in Volume 2, Page 1 of DeWitt Naturalization Record. This declaration states that he was born in Kreis Von Growentz, that he landed at the port of New York in April of 1870, that he was a subject of the Emperor of Prussia and that he was 73 years old. (That age matter may be the result of the language barrier.)

DeWitt County Deed Records show the following: On September 6, 1877, Katarina Kaminski purchased 40 acres of land in the J. W. Linan Survey Four miles north of Yorktown from John Skrobarczyk for $115. Skrobarczyk had purchased it from C. H. Heissig and wife Henriette on September 23, 1876 for $120.00 in coin. Heissig had bought 80 acres from the E. M. Edwards estate.

On October 24, 1881, Thomas Kaminski purchased 40 acres of land in the J.W. Linan survey four miles north of Yorktown (next to Katrina's 40 acres) from M. A. Hayen.

On November 18, 1907, Katrina Kaminski and the children of Thomas Kaminski transferred 150 acres in the J. W. Linan Survey to John Kaminski. In addition to John, the children were Katie Warzecha with husband August Warzecha, Frances Kozielski with husband Isidore Kozielski, all of DeWitt County, Isidore Kaminski and Agnes Pruski of Wilson County, Mary McKinney with husband John McKinney of Walker County and Stances Schroedter with husband Otto Schroedter of Bexar County. Transfer consideration was $2,400.00 cash and John had to provide for the care of Katrina for the rest of her life.

An interesting bit of information is that the 1880 census shows that Catherine (Katie) Kaminski was a servant in the household of August Birchoff who was a bookkeeper born in Bremen and was aged 33 with his wife, Alma, aged 23, and children Alma aged 4 and Alfreda aged 1 and mother-in-law, Caroline Rochow.

This Katie Kaminski was the mother of our subject, Vincent Warzecha. We will meet both of them later.

THE DRZYMALA FAMILY

Michael Drzymala and wife Frances Sadlacyk Drzymala with their children Julie, Elizabeth, and Annie arrived in Texas from Poland in 1877 or 1878. (I couldn't establish the exact time.)

There are a number of variations in the spelling of their name. Variations I ran across are: Drzymala, Drzemala, Dreymala, Drzimalla, Drzymata, and Drzemata.

The 1880 census for Bexar County lists this family on page 216:

Michael Drzimalla	age 30	Farmer	born in Prussia
Frances Drzimalla	age 30	Housewife	born in Prussia
Julia Drzimalla	age 7		born in Prussia
Elizabeth Drzimalla	age 5		born in Prussia
Annie Drzimalla	age 3		born in Prussia
Stephen Drzimalla	age 1		born in Texas

The tragic story of Michael's death was told by several family members who lived in San Antonio, namely Eleanor Gawlik, Louise Mingo, and Everett Dworaczyk. It was confirmed by Rose Nemietz, also of San Antonio.

Michael and Franceszka and children were living in St. Hedwig in Bexar County in September 1888. Michael witnessed a bank robbery by the Butler Brothers. He didn't report the information to anyone for fear of their reprisal since he was sure they knew him and knew he was a witness. That night when he was at home eating supper with his family, the Butler Brothers came to his home and called him outside. When he stepped out of the house, they shot him several times and left him for dead.

Franceszka was very frightened and she and the children loaded Michael and what belongings they could take on a wagon and drove through the dark to the more secure Polish settlement of Panna Maria. There they cared for him until he died 14 days later from gangrene. She and her children remained in the Panna Maria-Koscusko area the rest of her life.

Michael was buried in the cemetery at Immaculate Conception Church in Panna Maria. His grave marker shows his date of birth to be August 29, 1849 and his date of death as September 29, 1888.

Francesczka was buried in the cemetery at St. Ann's Church in Koscusko. Her grave marker shows her date of birth as April 12, 1851 and her date of death as November 7, 1916.

Drzymala family records show the children of this union to have been:

Julia	born 04-04-1872	died 03-06-1918
Elizabeth	07-07-1875	03-31-1956
Annie	1876	1946
Steve	12-26-1878	10-03-1942
Matthew	02-24-1882	09-02-1963
Pauline	06-20-1883	04-09-1944
Andrew	11-30-1884	01-31-1939
Sophia	05-05-1886	12-21-1963
Frances	1888	1963

Our principal subject, Susie, is a daughter of Steve whose family story we will read further on in this reflection.

THE SNOGA FAMILY

The fourth Polish immigrant family which were the corner posts for the foundation of our subject family was the Anton and Karolina Snoga family.

Anton and Karolina Leszczye Snoga and three children came to Texas from Poland in the 1875-1876 period.

The 1880 census for Wilson County show, on page 75:

Anton Snoga	white Male	37	Farmer	born in Strititz
Karolina Snoga	white F	31	Wife	born in Strititz
Karolina Snoga	white F	9	Dau.	born in Strititz
Julianius Snoga	white M	7	Son	born in Strititz
Paulina Snoga	white F	6	Dau.	born in Strititz
Peter Snoga	white M	3	Son	born in Texas
Louis Snoga	white M	10 M.	Son	born in Texas

It is not clear where this family came from. The name Strititz shows up in online search engines as a family surname rather than a location. Census records on other Snoga families show they came from Prussia, as many of the other Polish families did.

Wilson County Naturalization Records, Volume 4, Page 1 shows that Anton Snoga was born in Prussia. His Declaration of Intent was filed on November 4, 1879. His Petition For Citizenship was filed December 7, 1891. His citizenship was processed and approved by the Karnes County District Court.

In addition to the children named in the 1880 Census, Anton and Karolina had a daughter, Bena, who was born December 2, 1881 and a son, Vincent, born on January 22, 1887.

Bena Snoga is the mother of our subject, Susie Drzymala Warzecha.

Grave markers in the Catholic Cemetery at Kosciusko show the following information:

Anton Snoga	born 04-03-1845	died 09-04-1920
Karolina Snoga	born 06-23-1846	died 05-31-1920

THE WARZECHA-KAMINSKI UNION

On May 3, 1887, August Warzecha and Katerina Kaminski were married in the presence of Father John Hagel. Witnesses were Joseph Agnoni and Seaford Sidonia.

They made their home near the Sandies Creek about half way between the city of Cuero and the community of Lindenau on what is now called Wofford Lane off Farm Road 953 in DeWitt County. They worked a large farming and ranching operation with holdings in the Mustang Mott community and in the Fordtran area of Victoria County on the Chicolete Creek in addition to vast acreage on the homestead. Without exaggeration, they can be considered very successful members of the area.

To this couple were born seven sons who all grew to manhood. They were:

John August	born 02-03-1888	died 02-06-1978
August Steve	born 08-27-1889	died 12-12-1968
Benjamin Lawrence	born 08-13-1891	died 06-23-1934
Frank John	born 01-27-1894	died 01-12-1965
Joseph Theodore	born 03-17-1896	died 03-01-1972
Vincent William	born 04-04-1898	died 06-24-1987
Peter Paul	born 04-19-1906	died 02-08-1993

Three of their sons served in the U. S. Army during World War I. They were Benjamin, Frank, and Joseph, reflecting the patriotic service to their nation as displayed by their Grandfather, John Warzecha, during the U. S. Civil War.

August was a first generation citizen having been born in Panna Maria on August 18, 1859. He died December 3, 1942 of Chronic Degenerative Myocarditis and was buried in Hillside Cemetery in Cuero.

Katrina, known as Katie all her life, was born November 9, 1862 in Prussia (German Poland) and died November 18, 1937 of Hypostatic Pneumonia following fracture of her leg. She is buried along the side of her husband in Hillside Cemetery.

Their sixth son, Vincent, is the subject of this story.

THE DRZYMALA-SNOGA UNION

On Tuesday, October 8, 1901 Steve Drzymala and Bena Snoga pronounced their vows of marriage in the Catholic Church in Kosciusko with its pastor, Father W. Matysick as the church's official witness. And thus began a union which lasted until death separated them more than 40 years later.

The young couple settled in Denhawken where they were successful farmers. It was there that the first seven of their children were born. Helen, the baby of the family, was born in Yorktown. Their children were:

Henry	born 07-13-1902	died 01-04-1967
Susie	born 05-17-1905	died 10-28-1982
Fred	born 08-31-1907	died 12-06-1978
Frank	born 08-17-1909	died 01-13-1973

Herman	born 01-19-1912	died 06-18-1972
Irene	born 04-17-1914	died 08-09-2005
Stanley	born 05-12-1917	died 10-31-1980
Helen	born 11-07-1923	died 03-28-1985

In 1920, the family moved to Yorktown to a 227 acre farm they purchased about two miles east of town. Two years later, they traded the farm for the Yorktown Bottling and Ice Cream Works and the adjoining home owned by R. A. Randow.

It is from this family that our subject, Susie, came forth to become the matriarch of THE WARZECHAS OF MUSTANG MOTT.

CHAPTER THREE

AFTER THE BEGINNING

STORIES ABOUT THE VINCENT
AND SUSIE FAMILY

ADVICE

Rose remembers this advice she got from Mom and Dad: "One Sunday afternoon a bunch of boys and girls came over to the house. I guess they wanted me to go out with them, but I wasn't old enough to date yet. They stayed at our house for a while and started looking for some cards or dominoes to play. After a while, Dad came in the living room where we were and said there was to be no gambling in his house. That is why, until this day, I never play poker."

She also remembered: "When I started dating, I didn't know any boys except from Lindenau and Cuero. One day while cooking dinner or washing clothes, I can't remember, Mom had a talk with me and told me they would like me to go with some Polish boys from Yorktown. So we started going to Yorktown Community Hall for feasts and dances and, of course, I met a lot of Polish boys there. Over the years I met a lot of boys and on August 15, 1945 I guess I met the right one as we are still together after more than 50 years."

Newton recalls: "Dad gave very little advice, but when he did tell you something, you better listen carefully because he really meant it.

My advice story goes like this: "When I was in the Army and heading for an overseas assignment in Korea during that war, Mom and Dad both gave me some parting advice. Dad said that if I got into combat, I should remember to keep my head down. I suppose he thought if I got shot, it should be in the other end. Mom simply said that if I found any girls to go out with to remember to keep my pants zipped up. Also to write often and to pray every day.

No matter what the occasion was, their advice was always right on the mark.

ANIMAL FEED

Dad believed in utilizing every possible source of feed for the animals we raised. Hogs got weeds and grass from the yard and garden as well as vegetable scraps, coffee grounds and kitchen waste (slop was what we called it). When there was no grass for grazing (for example, in the winter), the cattle got hay we put up in the summer. When we kids were growing up, hay baling hadn't been developed yet so we cured the hay in the field and stacked it into piles called "shocks". Then we would drag those shocks to the hay lot behind the tractor or a team of mules. This was the kids' job while Dad and Vincent transferred these shocks into "hay stacks" which generally stood 10 feet or so tall and 10 to 12 feet in diameter. Vince had the hardest job because he had to toss that hay all the way up onto the pile as Dad was arranging it into a solid structure in an engineering masterpiece that wouldn't collapse. Sometimes Vince and Dad swapped jobs and Vince had to do the engineering part.

Truly a man's job for a young boy. To get the hay out of the stacks when it was time to feed it, we had to use a rod about 36 inches long fashioned with a hook on one end. We would ram this rod into the stack and pull hay from within the stack. It was a very ingenious tool that Grandpa Warzecha had made in his blacksmith shop according to Dad's specifications. I have this tool in my possession and have used it as a wall decoration and conversation piece.

To supplement this hay (generally made from sorghum cane), we cut and bundled corn tops. Corn stalks usually grew about 6 feet in height with the ear or ears near mid-point. While the stalks were still green, but the corn mature, we would cut off that portion of the stalk above the ears. These sections (called "corn tops") were laid in piles on the ground to dry. When cured by the drying process, we tied the piles into bundles which were then stored in the barn for winter feed. Putting up corn tops was our least favorite chore. When cutting the tops, we were scratched and cut many times by the naturally sharp edges of the corn leaves. Sometimes, we were also cut by the slip of our knives which had to be razor sharp to accomplish the job. While this phase of the job was undesirable, the tying of the bundles was down-right horrible. This task had to be performed when the dried stalks and leaves were damp with the dew so they wouldn't crumble. That meant starting this job as soon as there was enough light to find the piles. On a moonlit morning, that could be at 4 A.M. We had to disregard the possibility that a snake had sought refuge inside or under each and every pile, otherwise we would have been too frightened to do the job. Yet, we did find snakes occasionally, but we kept that news to ourselves so we wouldn't frighten one of our brothers because if one of us got scared and quit, the others had to work harder to pick up the slack. The string we used to tie the bundles was a rough hemp-like twine that promptly wore blisters on all our fingers. There was no such thing as wearing gloves for this tying job. It wasn't long before we were really hurting, but the job had to be done and a little thing like pain couldn't stop the work. As you know by now, none of us died from the hard work or bleeding blisters. The work had to be done. The family depended on everyone pulling his or her weight.

The chickens and turkeys got corn or whatever other grain was available. Sometimes we kids played tricks on the chickens by tying a grain of corn to a string and placing that grain in a pile of other corn. When a chicken swallowed that grain, we had us a chicken caught, or at least surprised as she could be. We thought that was a lot of fun. We got a few whippings for having our fun at the expense of the poor chickens.

We never tried that trick on turkeys. They were too big. The turkeys, in addition to eating grain, ate insects and grass seeds. It was my job for several years to herd the turkeys across the road into the Hamilton Ranch to graze on grasshoppers and other bugs. I would carry some water and a sack lunch as the turkeys and I would stay out all day. The only protection I was allowed to carry was a hoe with which to kill rattlesnakes and coral snakes. Non-poisonous snakes were spared, but we couldn't take the risk that one of the poisonous snakes would bite me or the turkeys.

By utilizing every available form of food for the animals, we were able to harvest enough produce to feed the family and pay all bills on time.

BUTCHERING

When the first good cold front (we called them northers because they came from the north), arrived in the Fall, it was time to butcher a hog and cure it. We would start by cleaning and filling the big cast iron wash pot with water and building a fire around it. While the water was getting hot, all kinds of preparations were being made. Mom and Rose prepared things in the house including getting pans ready for the meat, making room in the house and smokehouse to work the meat, getting out the pots and pans we needed and making sure the sausage stuffer and all the other utensils were clean and ready for use. Dad sharpened the knives while we kids chopped the wood for the fire and gathered the block and tackle needed to hoist the hog by its hind legs to disembowel it after the hair was scraped off with sharp knives. Vince was entrusted to get Dad's .22 caliber rifle and shells with which Dad would kill the animal. After proper bleeding was done, the hog was dragged to the wood pile for the scraping and dressing. With Mom and Dad's guidance, we all worked at various jobs until the meat was cut up as needed, sausage was made and the lard was rendered.

This was basically an all day project and we were exhausted at the end of the day. Mom and Rose would always prepare the day's meals from the fresh meat. Usually, for the noon meal (dinner to us) we would have fried liver and heart with mashed potatoes and whatever other vegetables were available. The evening meal (supper to us) consisted of fried sausage patties with home-made scratch biscuits and gravy or molasses. You couldn't find a better meal anywhere in the country.

After dark we sat around the fire to keep warm while we rendered the lard (boiled chunks of fat and grease to separate the fatty oil from the skin and membranes). Every now and then, we would fish out of the boiling fat a few pieces of crackling to cool so we could munch on them. And all the time, someone would get started telling jokes or scary stories or flat-out lies and everyone would try to top the others' stories. That was real living. What did the city folks know about life? Not much, from our way of thinking.

The day ended with the sausage hanging on sticks and rods over a smoke pot filled with wet corn cobs with hot coals on top to create the smoke with which the sausage was cured. It's no wonder that little house was called a smokehouse. While we kept a watch on the smoking process to prevent fire flare-ups, we cleaned up all the knives, cutting boards, pots, pans, tubs, floor in the wash room and all the utensils we used so everything could be put away clean before we went to bed for tomorrow would be a new day with new things to do.

Butchering day was one of the longest days for us because they never ended much before mid-night. When we went to bed, we were tired, every one of us.

Looking back on projects like this, it's clear to see that Mom and Dad were remarkable managers of people and with the outstanding help and support from Rose and Vince (the two oldest who carried the bulk of the work) we younger ones truly enjoyed a wonderful family life.

The grandchildren also remember the butchering process. Even though it was hard work, there was always some fun to be had.

Peggy directs, "Don't forget about butchering a hog and making sausage together. We always butchered chickens together, too. Now THERE is a lost art these days."

Cynthia recalls: I also remember making sausage every Thanksgiving. We had a real assembly line going. Mom and Aunt Dawn were cleaning casings, cutting them and tying the strings in the front room of the smokehouse. Uncle Tony was operating the stuffer and I was putting the casings on the stuffer. At one particular point, Uncle Bubba (Vincent) was in the front room and I was teaching Chris how to put the casings on. Simultaneously, I told Chris to 'stick your finger in it' to get the casing open to get it on the stuffer and Uncle Bubba passed some gas. The timing was perfect and we all had a good laugh. Those sure were fun times."

Sue Lynn has these thoughts: "Didn't everyone have the greatest time when the men would get together and butcher a hog? I was probably the most excited person when they would get the hog on that butchering table behind the house. Of course, I was going through my tomboy stages and I wanted to be like the other guys and do all those gory things with them. I remember seeing all the uncles in their old jeans and shirts and cowboy hats and just work together. That was a great tradition and I miss those hogs."

CATTLE

Dad raised cattle for income and had several herds. He had cattle at the Sandies Place and on the one he bought near Yorktown that we called the Henkes' Place because he bought it from a widow named Carolyn Henkes. He also had some cattle for a while on a rented place near Ratcliff and a few at the home place. It was always our joy after we left home to return and help him "work cattle." That consisted of doctoring, vaccinating, castrating, sorting, culling, and whatever else needed to be done.

He had many good cows and some ornery ones, but the meanest he ever had was a solid black Brahman crossbred cow with horns that stood almost straight up and were at least 18 inches long. It always seemed like those horns grew by leaps and bounds when she was chasing you. She would chase anything and anybody around and when she had a calf, look out!!! There were many times she put us up trees and over or under or through fences. She was something else!! When we asked Dad why he kept such a cow on the place, his response was very simple and logical, "because she raises the best calves on the place." He kept her at the Henkes place and as far as I know she stayed there from the time he bought her until the day he sold her.

A funny thing about him and that cow; I never saw her chase him. They had a special respect for each other.

The cows he kept at home doubled as milch cows and beef cows. We produced all the milk the family used until the later years when Mom and Dad bought milk from the store for their use.

We kids all learned how to gather the milk from the cows even though we sometimes got kicked and spilled a bucket of milk. Dad was a master at this, though, and it was fun to watch him squirt milk direct from the udder to the open mouth of a barnyard cat waiting for a handout.

CHARACTER

There are several stories that belong under this heading.

Vince says: "In response to a request for us to write something about Mom and Dad, there are many things that can be said. First of all, the thing that I think about a lot is how both Mom and Dad managed to have and raise seven children starting in the Depression and continuing until they had everyone out of school and gone on their own way. They were remarkable people."

Newton recalls: "Mom never said anything bad to me about anyone. She was a very kind and loving person."

Sue Lynn writes: "I cherished my time with Grandma, especially when I had her all to myself. I loved to sing around the yard and just to amuse myself. I remember singing one day and Grandma was in the house listening to my off-key tunes. Boy, I was terrible. I heard her clapping and I looked up to see her standing by an open window, just smiling broadly at me. Grandma had always encouraged me to sing, or do whatever my heart desired. It didn't matter that I didn't sing beautifully or that I was getting the words mixed up. It was then that I complained to Grandma that my singing was terrible and I wanted to know why I wasn't as good as other people were. She sat me down and explained that not everyone was a great singer, but that shouldn't prevent one from singing anyway. Grandma was quick to point out that I was very talented in other things and that there were people who weren't as good as I was. A few years ago, my mother gave me a book on wisdom that I continue to read through occasionally. It was one of the best gifts I have ever received. Recently, I came across a quote from that book and it reminded me so much of the lecture that Grandma had given me. It was something about how everyone should use their talents to their fullest even if they weren't the best. It makes the world a more colorful place to live in."

Carol: "I remember Grandma always seemed to be wearing an apron."

Gary offered these thoughts: "If there is one word I can use to describe Grandma and Grandpa, it would be generous. If they had something, you had something. I really respect the way they raised their kids (my father and my aunt and my uncles). They always had a lot of love for everyone. Another thing I remember about Grandma and Grandpa is how calm they were with us (the grandchildren). I remember one time Chris locked Carol and me in the old chicken coop and there were all those rat tails hanging out of the wall. We got scared and when we finally got out and told Grandpa, he acted like it was no big deal. I will always remember that."

Nancy had this to say: "They definitely had a pattern to their lives. Every day at noon they would listen to the news program on the local radio station. Then they would take a nap. Every Saturday night they would sit in front of the television and watch 'The Lawrence Welk Show'. I don't think they ever missed as episode and I bet if there were VCRs around when they were alive, they would have taped every episode and watched them daily."

Patsy says: "I guess what always stays with me is the sound of Pop's laugh. It was such a hearty, deep, real laugh that I can hear it to this day. He shared it with people real often. I remember the size of his hands. They were the hands of a man who knew lots of hard wotk and yet they were tender hands. I always called him Pop instead of Dad as he and I agreed on this name before my marriage to David. I remember when we went to tell him that we were planning to marry, he told me right off that from that day forward I would have to call him something besides Mr. Warzecha since I was to be part of the family.

I remember how much he liked flowers. He would really light up when we would go to visit and I would pick some flowers from our yard in town and take them to him. I can remember him getting flowers for his birthday one time and how happy and pleased he was. He liked simple things like that."

Mike has this story: "It was Thanksgiving 1975 and I was in college at Sam Houston State. I didn't have much money, but that's nothing new. I had gone to Cuero for the full week, figuring I could augment my meager rations with some venison along with enjoying a festive get together with most of the family. Mom, Dad and Chris arrived in time for the holiday at which time I still hadn't seen a buck anywhere. I kept going out every morning and evening looking. I went to the Sandies Place, the Henkes Place, the Saunders Place and still not a buck in sight.

Finally, Saturday evening I took Mom's van out to the edge of Grandpa's oats patch, next to the road into the house and bedded down for the night. Time was running out as I had to be in Huntsville on Monday morning for classes. I woke up Sunday morning about half an hour before sunrise and watched the field as darkness fled. After several minutes, I realized there were seven or eight deer in the field about 75 yards out, but I couldn't tell their gender without more light. I waited and watched the group and finally concluded they all were doe. I was about to leave in disgust when my stomach growled to remind me that the cupboards were bare back home. I stuck the barrel of my M-1 carbine out the window and fired. It was a direct miss. I raised my sights a notch and shot again. Bingo!! She crumpled, but the other six or seven just stood there, so I shot another one (they were pretty small and I was real hungry). I loaded them into the van, went back to the barnyard and got busy. By the time everybody got back from church, I had my carcasses dressed and the sex organs, heads and hooves buried.

Now this is where Grandpa comes into the story. When he realized that I had doe and not bucks, he started reading me the riot act for poaching. I explained that I knew the law, but needed the meat. I continued that I hoped the game warden was in church with them as usual and that I was careful about disposing of any incriminating evidence. Grandpa just looked at me, shook his head and said something like 'let's get after it.' First we skinned both animals and cut them in half, then carried them to the smokehouse for weighing and cutting. They were small only 22 to 26 pounds a side. Finally, I was ready for the last step, my first lesson in butchering. Grandpa proceeded to show me some common cuts, what their names were, what to keep, what to throw away and how to wrap it, pack it, and prepare it.

After loading the ice chest and saying my good-byes and thank yous, I jumped in the car and headed for Huntsville, with about seventy pounds of venison and an experience I'll never forget."

CHORES

Chores on the farm were a fact of life. Some recollections of them are as follows:

Rose: "We all worked in the cotton fields, chopping cotton in the early summer and picking cotton in the late summer. This was a very hard job for me. I wasn't very fast, but I was out there doing my best because I wanted to earn some spending money. We were paid 10 cents for each hundred pounds of cotton we picked and brought to the scale to weigh. We kids did a lot of picking by ourselves the year the house was being built. That was the year Bobby was born. We did have hired hands to help pick cotton when we had too much to pick ourselves."

Also, "Because there was no television, on rainy days when we couldn't work in the fields, we were sent to the corn crib to shuck corn and shell it for the chickens, turkeys, etc. That might have been just an excuse to get us out of the house when we were too noisy, but it sure kept us busy and helped get the chores done."

Lad: "What a terrible shame that not everybody has the chance to grow up on a farm with loving parents like God gave us. It's not that it was easy. Far from it. But they set an example of responsibility and they taught us responsibility. They didn't preach about it, they showed us."

And, "Chores. We all had them. Some gave rise to a certain amount of horseplay in the barn and sometimes the chickens got fed and the eggs gathered after the chickens had gone to bed, but it got done. And, the next day things were done more on time. It's funny, but thoughts of the barn remind me of the old corn kernel on a string stunt with the chickens and of once mounting a horse while he was lying down asleep. Boy, I now strongly advise against trying that."

CHRISTMAS

When we were growing up, Mom and Dad let us shoot fireworks at Christmas time while we waited for Santa Claus to come. It always happened that while we kids were outside shooting fireworks under Dad's watchful eye and Mom stayed in the house to clean up the kitchen after supper, Santa would slip into the house and leave some gifts for the children. At the appropriate time, someone would hear some noises in the living room and everyone would race into the house to try to catch Santa in the act. We never were fast enough. He made his escape every time, EXCEPT one time after we were grown up and the same procedure was followed for the benefit of the grandchildren. That time, Santa WAS caught in the act. The little ones never knew that Anna Warzecha, a neighbor and cousin of Dad, was under that suit. She laughed a lot about that and said the beard sure did tickle her face.

After the 'Christmas tree' gift opening, we all got ready to go to Midnight Mass at St. Michael Church in Cuero. Since everyone always got practical gifts (items of clothing), we were well dressed for that Mass. Never mind that when we were kids, we generally slept through most of that late hour Mass, but we did pray and we did attend Mass and we were well dressed.

Christmas Day was always a big feast day. Mom prepared a huge meal with at least three kinds of meat and a half dozen kinds of vegetables with homemade bread and cake or pie for dessert. Rose and then the daughters-in-law helped Mom with the chores. That was a time for visiting as well as meal preparation. Mom ran a tight kitchen with each helper having a specific job to perform. They turned out many a delicious meal.

There was never a kid, little or big, who attended one of Mom and Dad's Christmases who could forget it.

Peggy has this recollection: "Christmas was always special. The living room always looked like a kid's dream of Christmas. The many gaily decorated presents all along the wall and around the tree. Great food! Cookies and other treats were on the corner table. Family all around opening presents and getting to catch up on what was happening to each other. I have such wonderful memories of these good times."

Sometimes these gatherings meant the introduction of new family members to the rest of the family either by marriage or by birth. It was in 1979 that another member named Sue met the family. That was Mike's wife of seven months. Previous entries, of course, were Mom (Susie), Sue Lynn, and Susan Tam. Another would join the family when Newton married Suzi. It's no wonder that these Christmas gatherings became such important occasions. Dad continued the tradition after Mom died, even though it was devastating to him to not have her there with him. We all missed her, but we knew he took it the hardest. We all tried to make the occasions festive for his benefit because we knew what joy the two of them had always gotten out of this time of the year which they devoted to the little ones.

Christmas was always directed to bringing joy and happiness to the children. And Mom and Dad were specialists in doing that.

COOTIES

When I was in the first grade, Rose, Vincent, Lad and I went to Guilford School, which was just off the Cuero-Westhoff highway (US 87 now). We rode horses and went through the neighbors' places to and from school. Even so, it was about four miles each way. It was on one of these trips that old Paint got spooked by a rabbit and threw Rose off breaking her arm. She was in a cast and sling for the required healing time and received the proper amount of sympathy.

One time when I thought I ought to get sympathy, I got none. Mrs. A. W. (Isabella) Shaffner was my teacher. She was a highly respected, dignified, refined, kind and gentle soul. One day when she was performing hygiene inspections, she discovered I had head lice (cooties). Most of the kids in my class did too, but that sure didn't make my situation any more acceptable. Mrs. Shaffner thought enough of my folks that she personally drove me home to console Mom instead of simply sending a note home like she did with the rest of the kids. (Maybe the fact that Dad was on the School Board of Trustees had something to do with it.) Well, you can imagine Mom's humiliation when Mrs. Shaffner dropped her bombshell. Right away, Mom got some hot water, a slab of her homemade lye soap and some turpentine. With these ingredients, she proceeded to get rid of the lice while Mrs. Shaffner kept her company and consoled her. Mom did such a good job getting rid of those pests that I never had lice again. I also don't have much hair now, but I doubt that the lye soap and turpentine had anything to do with it.

DAD'S MUSTANG GRAPE WINE

Dawn recalled this story about Dad's homemade wine:

"When we were living in Friendswood, Tony decided to make some homemade wine. He set up his wine making operation in a corner of the breakfast room. His results were not nearly as high as his expectations so I asked Dad for his wine making recipe. In his own handwriting Dad gave us these instructions:

'Crush grapes real good. You may add one or two pints of water to each gallon of mash. Let stand for 8 to 10 days or until juice is clear. Drain out and add two and a half or three pounds of sugar to each gallon of juice and dissolve. Fill container full so that it can throw off any impurities while it is fermenting. Do not close the container tight until it is through fermenting.'

Everybody always liked his wine made from the purple wild mustang grapes that were so plentiful on his places on the Sandies Creek and at Yorktown. I liked it but when a little bubbly soda water was added it seemed so sweet to me."

See more on this matter under the heading "Drinking".

DAD'S SHOP

Lad has this wonderful memory:

"Dad's workshop (I don't know why we called it simply the 'shop', not the 'workshop') was not only an indispensable workplace, but also a major storage facility, a place of adventure and a place for learning. Spare parts from old farm tools, bent nails to be straightened and used again as well as new ones, carpentry tools with a bit of mileage on them, but very useful and used, saddles, bridles, saddle blankets, carbide possum hunting headlights, axes, drop augers, crow bars, that marvelous big hand cranked drill press, screen wire, bolts, nuts, cotton picking sacks, kneepads, and a thousand other useful items could be found in there. It was the kneepads that reminded me of the SHOP this morning. On my back on the basement floor doing some exercises, I looked up and saw that pair of kneepads hanging on the wall; kneepads from Dad's shop. I'm sure they're too new to be some of those I used before I left home, but somebody in the family put a bunch of miles on them. Dad let me take them to hang on our wall at a time when I thought my job at GE was pretty tough. Boy, they reminded me that my job was easy in comparison. But the shop was the scene of a lot of projects: chicken coops, rabbit traps, shoe shine boxes, etc. And some things went on behind it too! One of our brothers is known to have buried out of season carcasses there, all of the brothers are known to have used the area as a stand up latrine. But the shop is also the place where we got a lot of hands-on teaching from Dad in doing projects and learning lots of skills we needed on the farm. He trusted us to use his shop tools and he tolerated the mistakes we made. And that's the part that's most memorable about Dad's Shop."

Mike, too, has memories of that shop:

"Grandpa's shop was THE most wonderful place I ever saw and I mean it was full of wonder. How any place could contain so many interesting things is beyond me. The thing that intrigued me the most was the drill press mounted on the wall. I sure would like to have one like that as a reminder of the things Grandpa kept in there."

DAD'S STERNNESS

Dad could be gentle and kind, as he generally was, but he could also be firm and unyielding. The following recollections are testimony to that:

<u>Vincent</u>: "Dad used to plant beans between the rows of corn after the corn had grown six or eight feet tall and was nearly mature. First of all, he would run a three shovel plow down the row to clean the weeds and grass out and to loosen the ground. This was pulled by one mule. Right behind that operation came the walking planter pulled by one mule. Each of these operations required a person to handle the mule and implement. When I was ten or eleven years old, Dad thought I was big enough to handle the planter. I weighed 80 or 90 pounds and that's not much when it comes to controlling a big mule. Since I was Dad's son, I drew that responsibility, though, a hired hand's son who weighed 50 or 60 pounds more than I did and was a couple of years older was assigned the three shovel job. Well, the planter turned over and I couldn't stand it up. I drove the mule and dragged the planter home. Dad saw the mess that was making of the corn in the field and he met me at the end of the field. I had already decided I'd rather leave home and promptly told him so. Needless to say, I didn't leave home because I couldn't sit for a week and could hardly walk. He took the plow lines and beat the hell out of me and then went and patted the mule. I didn't get to quit working that night until around nine o'clock and then I had to give that mule six extra ears of corn so he could walk fast the next day."

Newton: "After Dad bought the Henke place, he started planting cotton there as well as at home. One of the families who used to pick cotton for us was the Cisneros family. The parents were good workers, but the children weren't worth a hoot. One year Dad had some of them including a son and another woman picking cotton at the Henke place. He caught them making love in the field and ordered them off the place. They had to walk back to Cuero."

Newton continued: "I will never forget the talk Dad gave to the Lindenau School bus driver one time at Mustang Mott. It seems the driver always picked up us first and his daughter last, but he would take her home first and we were the last to get home. That meant we left for school in the dark and got home in the dark during the winter. After Dad's talk with that driver, he changed the schedule."

I might add that common sense dictated that the bus route should return the students in the same order as they were collected. Dad was on the Lindenau School Board with some influence over school matters and that helped settle the route issue. In all things, though, he rarely left a person wondering what he meant when he said anything.

Vince again: "There are a lot of stories we could tell, but the main thing is 'I miss them both'."

DANCING

Mom and Dad loved to dance. They would go to dances and celebrations which generally included music and a place to dance. They would really get going on a good polka, waltz, one-step, two-step, or schottische, but their favorite was the waltz. They made a beautiful couple on the dance floor and were in great demand by their friends as dance partners.

Dancing was such a natural part of their celebrations that when Rose and Tony got married, Dad had a dance floor platform built in the outer yard so everyone could dance. The Drzymala kinfolks brought their instruments and played all night long while everyone danced, partied and drank beer. That was when poor Rose bumped into a yard fence post in the excitement of the evening and was heard to say, "Excuse me!" We'll never let her live that down.

It just seemed normal that any significant celebration or social function should include music and dancing. I truly believe the folks were greatly disappointed that we boys could neither play any musical instruments nor dance.

Patsy relates this memory: "I remember the dancing ability of Pop. He was one of the world's best dancers of the waltz. Watch out Fred Astaire when Vincent Warzecha is on the scene. From visiting with him, it seems that he and Mrs. Warzecha loved to waltz and would do so every possible dance."

Patsy sure had that right.

(Mom had already died before Patsy came into David's life.)

DISHES

Doing the dishes after the evening meal was always the job for us kids. I remember some of the tricks we tried in an effort to dodge this duty, but Mom was always onto us. Poor Rose was always stuck with the washing job while we boys had to clear the table and then dry the dishes and put them away. One favorite trick was an urgent call of nature. Before we got indoor plumbing, this required a trip to the outhouse and in the dark we weren't so inclined to use this excuse, but after indoor plumbing arrived, we tried often to try it. One time I remember locking myself in the bathroom and crawling into the bathtub for a nap. Boy, did I catch it when Mom found out where I was. The main thing I remember about this is I never tried it again.

Another favorite ruse was the homework excuse. We had to be careful with this one since Mom started having the older ones quiz the younger ones, usually me. One time I thought it would be good to have to study my catechism lessons in preparation for First Communion. Well, Mom solved that by telling Rose to question me on my lessons while she washed and Brother (that's what we called Vince for many, many years), Ladis and I dried the dishes. Rose didn't like this too much as that meant she had to remember all the right questions to ask and then know if I had answered them correctly, but she always had the others to help her out. Generally, she'd start with the first question in the book: "Who made you?" I'd reply, "God made me." Then came "Why did God make you?" "To know him and to love him." "That's not the way the answer starts out. Try it again like it says in the Catechism." "God made me to know him and to love him and to serve him and my neighbor in this world and to be happy with him forever in the next." "That's good!" we heard Mom say from somewhere nearby. Then, "Go on with the next question," Mom would say. Rose would hesitate as if she was trying to remember what the next question was, but she had them all memorized by now since she had already put Brother and Ladis through this routine ahead of me. "To whose image and likeness did God make you?" was the next one. "God made me to his image and likeness." Sometimes the recitation was on prayers: "Say the Our Father." "Our Father, uh, whoartinheavenhallowedbyThyname . . ." "STOP THAT RIGHT NOW!!!" Mom would break in "AND SAY IT RIGHT. JUST LIKE YOU'RE TALKING TO GOD." Sometimes I wasn't very smart, but I did learn fast how to answer the questions and how to address my elders, even my older sister.

There were other lessons we learned while doing the dishes, besides how to do the dishes. That, in itself, took some instructions. If you were washing, you cleaned everything off the plates and pots and pans and things, dried food on the forks was especially hard to get off. If the washer missed something, the dryers generally called it to the washer's attention, unless Mom or Dad was the washer. If you were drying, you got everything good and dry and if your cloth got too wet, you traded it for a dry one. And when you were putting things away, you had to be real sure you put things where they belonged; no fair putting them somewhere just to get them off the drain board. A matter of accountability came into play here as Mom would always track down the culprit when mistakes were made.

Spelling was an exercise we could do while we were drying and one that we put to good use. Vince did a good job of giving the words to spell and he always knew the correct spelling. I think he always won the spelling bees at school.

Lad worked me over on my Arithmetic lessons since he was so good on Math. Multiplication tables had to be memorized and it was so much easier to memorize part of them and develop quick ways to figure out the rest. For example, you could run through the "nine times" table real quickly if you simply added nine to the answer for the previous problems as long as you were doing them in order. When you got into double digits times double digits, you reduced the problem to two or more smaller problems. Practicing these tricks with each other when doing chores sharpened our skills and allowed us to excel in the classroom.

It's no wonder we did well in school resulting in the reputation that "those Warzecha kids sure are intelligent."

I always thought that one of the ways Dad showed his love for Mom and his concern for her welfare was when he took over the dish washing chore after all the kids left home. Mom had such a bad allergic reaction on her hands from the detergent that she couldn't do the dishes without using gloves or sustaining a severe rash. Even though he had put in a hard day outside, he wasn't too "macho" to help her in the kitchen.

I remember that he would take the dish washing detail even when the children and grandchildren gathered for a big dinner. It was his way of showing Mom and us how he felt about her. There was one rule he followed and he expected the dish-dryers to honor. That was to not call his attention to anything he missed. He tried very hard to get things right, but he didn't like attention being called to anything he missed. The first person to complain about his efficiency got to replace him at the sink.

I always liked that philosophy.

DRIVING

Mom never learned to drive a car and wasn't interested in doing so. She always said there were enough drivers in the family already without running the risk of tearing up a car. We pooh-poohed that idea naturally. She still wouldn't relent. When we really pressed her about the matter, she finally admitted that she tried to learn to drive before she and Dad married and the experience scared the fool out of her. She said she tried to drive her father's delivery truck at the bottling and ice cream works and she hit the building. She said that frightened her so much she never tried again and she didn't plan to in the future. End of that subject!!!

Rose has this story about driving: "When I was old enough to get a driver's license, I drove Mama places she wanted to go. I remember one day, Mom, Grandma Drzymala and I went to Yorktown in the Model

A to go shopping. We had bought a bushel basket of peaches or pears, I can't remember which. Coming home, an old man didn't stop from a side street, so I hit him in the side, which knocked over his coop of chickens and he had chickens running all over town. Because it was the man's fault, he did not call the police, so we had our car towed to a garage and he paid to have it repaired, which probably cost him all of $16 or $18 and we had a rumble seat full of scattered peaches or pears, whichever it was.

DRINKING

In our family, it seems that alcohol was a normal part of life. There was never an abusive use of alcohol or prolonged heavy drinking even though we did drink on any occasion that seemed to merit a drink. Dad made some of the best homemade wine from wild muscadine grapes we called "mustang" grapes in honor of the wild horse and probably, from misunderstanding the term "muscadine."

Anyway, Dad followed the recipe passed on to him from his father. The grapes had to be picked at the height of their ripeness and washed in clean fresh water to remove as much of the spider webs, bird droppings, dust, and other pollutants as possible. Then the grapes were crushed in a wooden barrel using a wooden mallet or axe handle or other wooden instrument. You had to be careful not to introduce any metallic objects to the process as the reaction to the acid in the grapes would alter the taste. After the grapes were thoroughly crushed, you add one or two pints of clean water for each gallon of mash and let it stand for eight or ten days until the juice is clear. During this process, any trash or debris like leaves and stems will rise to the surface. Removing these as they settle in top will enhance the clarity of the juice. When the juice has become clear, drain it off into another clean wooden barrel and dissolve two and a half to three pounds of granulated sugar per gallon of juice. Fill the barrel full with this solution so any impurities will spill over the rim during the fermenting process. It is necessary to keep the container covered to prevent anything from entering the solution, but the cover must allow overflow of impurities to occur. This fermenting process will continue until, generally the first frost when the enzymes causing the fermentation will die. The wine is then ready for consumption. It will be a sweet burgundy with a slight zip to it, roughly 18% alcohol. Savor the bouquet as you sip it and allow it to float over the taste buds before swallowing it.

Vince offers these thoughts on drinking: "I think that today I finally realize why I like to have a drink of whiskey every so often. When we were small, it seems that I was always sick. Maybe I wasn't sick so much, maybe I pretended once in a while. Mom always gave a double dose of castor oil for whatever ailed a person, but she would also find a sip of bourbon to give afterwards. Maybe I was just trying for the sip. It was amazing how Mom and Dad could stretch things. A bottle of liquor would last a whole year way back then."

Newton remembers a story with a different twist: "When I was in high school, we always went to dances on Saturday nights. We may have not danced very much, but we did drink some beer. One day when I was in the barn shucking corn, Dad came in and said, 'I know that you and your friends are drinking beer when you go out. Just remember, if you get thrown in jail, you got yourself in and you will have to get yourself out'. END OF CONVERSATION."

I add this thought about drinking: "For many years, I enjoyed drinking. Often there was companionship as friends got together for a few drinks. Sometimes there was the need to find a way to relax after a troubling day at work and once I even had my cardiologist suggest I have a glass of wine or two each evening after my first heart attack. But, as time went on, I became dependent on alcohol for it IS an addictive drug for some people. In 1992, I submitted myself to an alcohol treatment program and was successful, through the grace of God, in overcoming my addiction. At this writing, I have twenty years of 'ONE-DAY-AT-A-TIME' sobriety and am grateful for the support of my family and the grace of God for this recovery."

EASTER

Peggy reminds us of Easter gatherings with these thoughts: "Easter was a special time, like Christmas. With all the kids going on the big green trailer to pick flowers for our Easter nests, then coming back for a big egg hunt."

Easter always was a big event with Mom and Dad. Being the major feast day of the Catholic Church, it represented a day of great joy and rejoicing. The Resurrection of Our Lord was indeed a time to celebrate. The penitential season of Lent was over and it was a time that we Catholics felt spiritually cleansed. Added to the religious nature of the season was the onset of Spring which signaled the renewal of life. The trees were in bud or leafing out, flowers were in bloom (by some phenomena of nature, the wildflowers were always in the height of their glory at Easter time), the fields were planted, the grass had greened up, new calves and pigs were being born and all manner of life was in abundance. It truly was a time to rejoice.

Unless you got as unlucky or as foolish as I did three years in a row. When we lived in Conroe, we were very active in the activities in our parish. Dawn sang in the choir, Mike was an altar boy, and I was a Minister of the Eucharist. It never failed that we were involved in these activities on Easter Sunday. At the same time, it never failed that Mom and Dad had arranged a big dinner at their house following Mass at St. Michael Church in Cuero and we were expected to be there for dinner. Well, to make a long story short, the Highway Patrolman in Schulenberg caught me three Easter Sundays in a row driving too fast to try to get to the folks for dinner after we did our duties in Conroe. That was one of the prices we paid for continuing the traditions the folks set up.

EDUCATION

Mom and Dad taught us kids the lessons of honesty, integrity, responsibility, faith, hard work, cooperation with each other, discipline, thrift, respect for others and all the other desirable qualities youngsters needed in their growing up process.

They believed very strongly in us getting an education and encouraged each of us to get as much education as we wanted or thought we needed to make our way in the world. Their lessons and encouragement paid dividends for each of us.

When Lad and I each graduated from high school and went to college, we were each only sixteen years old. Lad was better prepared and more mature than I was. He completed his Bachelor of Science in Electrical Engineering at age nineteen, a remarkable achievement by anyone's standards. I struggled, floundered and was unsure of myself. At age nineteen, I quit college and joined the army to win the war in Korea. I never finished my degree. I had too many changes in degree plans and I never really learned how to study and to master the college courses.

Newton and Bob each completed their degree plans; Newton with a B.S. in Petroleum Engineering and Bob with a B.S. in Agricultural Engineering.

The folks never gave up on any of us or on themselves. Even though their formal educations were limited, they never passed up an opportunity to learn something new. Whenever they had a chance they read current magazines and newspapers to learn more about their jobs and responsibilities. Testimony to their devotion to education was the fact that Dad was, for many years, a trustee of the Guilford and Lindenau schools which we attended. These were elected jobs without pay, elected by the parents of the students attending those schools. That was a reflection of how high the people of the community regarded them.

Rose recalls this: "I didn't finish high school because I stayed at home to help Mom with the washing and ironing for all those boys so they could go to school. I worked at J.C. Penny's on Saturdays for $2.50 per day."

It wasn't our idea that we should always be so spiffy looking with our pants and shirts always ironed, but Mom insisted that she wasn't going to have any of us looking sloppy.

Lad says this: "Mom and Dad had a passion for our education, that we could make the most of our talent and somehow lead an easier life than they had. I remember that they made sure we did our homework, kept track of our grades, etc.

But they were more involved than that. They knew our teachers a lot better than I knew my children's teachers. In fact, some of them became lifelong family friends, like Mrs. Shaffner, Mrs. Lueddeke, etc. And I recall Dad's serving on the School Board at Lindenau and Guilford. They took it seriously.

I was fortunate for the educational opportunity they gave me. And I know it was hard for them and perhaps for others in the family as well. I appreciate that. Dad once thought he'd like to see me go to Law School at Notre Dame. But it wasn't any big problem when I went another direction. I know now that I was better as an engineer than I would have been as a lawyer and I'm glad they were able and interested and encouraged me to study."

ENTERTAINING MOM AND DAD

Lad has this story:

"Perhaps a year or so before Mom passed away, we persuaded her and Dad to come to visit us in Pennsylvania. At the time we didn't really understand how much Mom's mobility was limited by her hip condition. We wanted to show them a good time. Some things worked and others didn't. The ride to Pennsylvania Dutch country was fun, seeing the Amish farmers with their horse drawn machinery on those beautiful rolling hillsides. The drive through Valley Forge Park where Washington and his troops had spent that terrible winter was interesting. We overdid it when we tried to visit Independence Park and the Liberty Bell in downtown Philadelphia. Mom didn't complain much, but we realized she couldn't walk as much as that excursion demanded, so we cut it short, had lunch someplace and came home. But we did have one outing that was special fun. Roy Clarke was playing at the Valley Forge Music Fair, a local theater/concert hall. It was not a terribly big place, but it has a revolving stage so that everyone gets to sit up fairly close. Yes, they had heard of Roy Clarke, seen him on HEE-HAW and thought they might like it. He put on a great show, played six or seven different instruments in a very high energy performance. To us it seemed like it was a special concert he was doing because it was something Mom and Dad would enjoy. We had a great time that night. One of those memories for a lifetime."

Carol, too, has a memory of a visit: "I remember Grandma and Grandpa visiting us in Pennsylvania and Grandma sitting on the couch crocheting lace. The same lace that would be added to the pillow cases given out at the family gathering shortly before Grandma died."

ENTREPRENEURSHIP ON THE FARM

Here are some thoughts from Lad:

"Entrepreneurship on the farm is using big words the mean 'trying to earn a living and make a better life for yourselves and your family.'

That may not be a good title for this little story, but it tells a big story itself, and I acknowledge that I had help from Elinor, Tony and Dawn in discussing these ideas. I hope they and others will help to elaborate and complete this story.

Recently Elinor and I were driving through the farm country of North Carolina on our winter trek from Pennsylvania to Florida when it occurred to me that Mom and Dad had engaged in a terrifically varied set of activities in earning a living on the farm. You may think of farm life as uncomplicated, simple, routine; busy summers, slow winters, every year the same as last year. Well, it might have been that way in some worlds, but not in the world where we grew up and saw our parents work for a better current and later life. I'm not sure they consciously thought of it as working for a better life. It could have been simply a survival instinct, but I'm convinced they were more forward looking and divinely inspired than most other people.

When I was a kid, I remember, the big income source for the family was cotton, picked by hand mostly by the family, although there was help from hired hands brought in for the day and by sharecroppers and rent hands living on the farm. And I'm sure everybody in the family know how much fun I think picking cotton is, even though the concept of trying to pick more than your big brother, Vincent, did (which I failed every single day) was a challenge hard to sidestep.

The more interesting story lies in the variety of cash producing activities that Mom and Dad brought to market over the years. I say 'Mom and Dad' because that's the way it was. They were both involved very actively, very much as today's two-wage-earner families.

Beyond raising cotton, the list includes:

> Raising and selling hogs.
> Raising and selling chickens and eggs.
> Raising and selling turkeys.
> Growing, harvesting and selling peanuts.
> Growing and selling various vegetables.
> Raising and selling cattle.
> Selling wool from the sheep raised for food.
> Growing and selling corn and other grain crops.
> Growing and selling hay from grass crops.
> Harvesting and selling pecans from the Sandies Place.

This list is incomplete due to memory failures, but it does paint a picture of a family occupied with a wide variety of income producing activities."

Typing the above thoughts from Lad brings to mind another major source of income for the family and that was the production of cream and butter. I have vivid memories of the cow milking process and the cooling of the milk and running it through the separator which separated the cream from the milk. The milk then went into the feed for the hogs and chickens while the cream went to town to the creamery and/or into butter which we kids churned with a hand operated butter churn. Mom and Rose then took the butter and pressed it into one pound blocks which were wrapped and sold to the grocery store for resale to the public. Dad's records, which I studied as research for this book, showed that in 1937, the cream account brought in $28.85 for the year. Every little bit helped with the job of providing for a growing family.

FAMILY BIRTHS

Here are some more recollections from Lad:

"There were obviously a bunch of family births in our house. Some I recall, some I don't. Well, I don't really recall the births, but do recall related events.

Like Newton's birth. I recall the new overalls that we (Vince, Tony and I) had for the car ride we took with Dad to get Grandma Drzymala, and the doctor or to just get us out of the house, I'm not really sure. Anyway, it was a beautiful day and we wore new overalls. We got a nice new brother, too. Or was that Tony's birth. Or maybe Bobby's. I'm not sure. BUT I am sure about those new pants.

Then Tony Tam brought Rose home for Virgie's birth. I remember going into the front bedroom and being amazed to see our sister breast feeding her newborn. What a sight that was!"

FAMILY NEWS CHANNEL

Some more thoughts from Lad:

"Mom and Dad were the most faithful news channel you've ever seen. NBC, CBS, CNN, etc. could have learned loads from them.

Whenever we talked with them, they'd tell us the family news. What was happening; who was what. How the grandchildren were doing, etc. There were never any editorials, no gossip, no scandals, no talking about the brothers and sister, no saying who got drunk or was getting fat or needed to shave or get a haircut or who owed them money or anything like that. How many parents are like that?"

Nancy chimes in: "Grandma and Grandpa kept in touch with everyone. Grandma kept every letter they received and she would share them with anyone who came to visit them. After Grandma passed away, Papa still kept in touch and he would write quite often. I miss their letters and I miss them greatly."

FAMILY TEAMWORK

In 1944, we made a bumper crop of cotton and corn. Dad had planted 22 acres of cotton and about the same in corn. We made up our minds that we would complete the entire harvest without any outside help. All of us were still at home. In fact, this was the last summer that we would all be at home together. By next summer, the outside world started laying claim to our lives, one by one we headed off to follow the call of our individual destinies.

As soon as school was out for the summer, we commenced to picking cotton. We picked 20 bales, and when I say we picked, that's what I mean. In those days, we completely separated the cotton fluff from the hulls. The gins were not equipped to accept cotton in the hulls at that time though we had heard that some of the more modern ones in West Texas could. Anyway, picking cotton was hard work, no matter how you did it. And Dad always insisted that we pick the cotton clean; get all the lint available on the stalk and keep trash out of the lint. That's how he always got top dollar for the harvest.

Rose generally took care of the housework and meals and laundry and outdoor chores in addition to taking care of David who was just under three years old. Included in this task was providing the field workers with a snack and drinking water around mid-morning and again in the middle of the afternoon. Her contribution in this way was invaluable because it freed up Mom and the boys in the field.

Vince (or Brother, as we called him in those days) was 17 years old and our leader in the field as we picked nearly a bale a day. Dad was usually on the road to or from the gin in Lindenau getting the cotton processed. We worked from early in the morning until generally 10 PM when we came in for supper. We made particularly long days when there was a bright moon to give us light. Mom and the boys spent long days in the hot sun, but we got the job done. Dad also helped in the fields for he was no slacker. Try as we might, even the best of us on our best day found it hard to stay up with him in the 'hard work' department. This remained true even into his later years.

While Dad was waiting his turn to get his cotton ginned, he caught up on the news or met with other men on the School Board on school business since he was on the Board of Trustees of the Lindenau School. He utilized every moment to its maximum capacity at all times.

In less than thirty days, we harvested the entire cotton crop without any loss to wind or rain damage. One day Vince picked over 400 pounds, Lad over 300 and I right at 200. Most other days we came close to those figures, but those were our top productions.

When we finished with the cotton, we took off for a day of fishing and swimming in the Sandies Creek. We couldn't squander any time, though, as there was always the threat of wind and rain storms that could ruin a crop in a hurry.

Then, we went to work on the corn crop, pulling every ear by hand and tossing it into the trailer pulled by the tractor driven by Bob who was not yet seven years old. Vince (17), Lad (15), I (13), and Newton (only 9) filled the trailer and delivered it to Dad at the barn. He unloaded it while we took the wagon and filled it. This assembly line harvest went on all day, every day except Sunday, until we had the entire crop in the barn.

It was during this time that the pilot trainees from Brayton Field at Cuero were training in their earnest. They were in their primary flight training flying PT-19s and would buzz our fields at such low altitudes we could see the smiles and bewilderment on their faces as some wondered what we were doing. We figured those that smiled and waved probably knew what we were doing while the others were simply getting an education. Occasionally, we would see one go below the horizon and just as we expected to hear the explosion of a crash, the plane would zoom up into the air and we could almost hear the joy and thrill of the pilot's excitement.

Those were good times for kids to be growing up.

FIRST CHRISTMAS AWAY

Lad recalls his first Christmas away from home:

"If you've never felt lonely or had doubts about yourself for a situation you've gotten yourself into, try Christmas Eve on a bitterly cold night in Pittsfield, Massachusetts when you're nineteen and have spent your previous eighteen Christmases with Mom and Dad plus Rose and your brothers doing fireworks, going to Confession, having a meatless meal, opening presents, taking a nap before Midnight Mass, putting on a new Christmas shirt or whatever, etc. What a wonderful memory Mom and Dad gave us with those Christmases. Of course, the gifts were always mostly practical things like shirts, shoes, neckties, etc. But there were always toys, too. Who can forget the year they decided to test our musical talents with the guitar I still have, Vince's accordion and Tony's violin. It seemed like a reasonable proposition, considering the musical talent in Mom's family, but it just didn't work. And I remember the Christmas trees. We used to go with Dad to the pasture to pick out a nice one, but not so nice that it might grow up to be a good fence post if we left it alone.

Those Christmases were really special, and here I was alone in Pittsfield. My roommate had gone home for the holidays, but I couldn't afford the trip to Texas. To salve the wound, a package came from Mom and Dad with a shirt or pajamas or something and some of Mom's cookies. Mom's cookies healed many aches and pains, no matter what their origin was. She probably wanted me home as badly as I wanted to be there, but that's one of those things we never talked about. Shame on me for that!

I survived that first Christmas and I guess it was part of the growing up or hardening process that young people must endure. After that first year, I was eligible for vacation, and whenever I could, I made it home for Christmas."

I, Tony, can really relate to that story from my own experiences. In 1951, I was in the Army headed for the Far East with a furlough at home in early December. I had to report to Camp Stoneman near San Francisco by mid-month for processing and shipment overseas. While I was at home on leave, we had my Christmas, but it's just not the same in the middle of the month as it is on the correct day with all the religious celebrations, etc. On December 20th, I sailed for Japan, the first member of our family to go overseas. It was a time of great uncertainty and apprehension. It just seemed so heartless and un-caring of the military to ship young men away from their homes at a time like this to a war from which many would not return, but war is hell and un-caring and there were men on the battlefield who were dying and replacements were badly needed. War does not know justice or play favorites or care about holidays or peoples' feelings or even their lives.

We spent Christmas and New Year's in the middle of the Pacific Ocean with only our memories and our personal thoughts to remind us of what we left behind. And we each knew that many of us would never see our loved ones again. Those were lonely days, but all the fellows on the ship had basically the same cares, fears, doubts and hopes and we consoled each other with thoughts of better times in the future.

The next two Christmases were also spent away from home, with 1952 being in a Quonset barracks in Taegu, Korea and 1953 being on a troop train between the Port of Embarkation at Seattle, Washington and Ft. Bliss at El Paso, Texas where I was going to be discharged from the Army. There is no way to say that these two were any easier to be away from home than the first except with the thought that you will never have to repeat the earlier sad and lonely feelings of spending Christmas while you are going away. It's hard to explain, but when you are going away from something like happy times, it is much harder to handle than when you have already been away from it for some time.

At any rate, your first Christmas away from home is not a happy time.

FISHING

How could this collection of stories be complete without some on fishing? Well, we just have a few.

Lad tells this one and it's not just about fishing:

"Dad had always done everything he could for us, not just as kids, but in later years as well. A couple of big disappointments came when I thought I would entertain him. Once, after Mom had taken her place in Heaven, he was visiting us in Pennsylvania for a short while. I spent some days working and some vacationing. I decided to take him fishing to local lakes and reservoirs where Gary and I had fished. Dad and I didn't catch a thing. Maybe a tick or two, but that's all. A year or two later we were visiting Dad in a time when he was making daily trips to Victoria for radiation treatments. I drove him several times and decided that one day it would be fun to go fishing in the afternoon. Gary was with us. We drove to Victoria. Dad got his treatment. We drove to Rockport or Port Aransas or someplace, I can't recall. We had lunch. Then we chartered a fishing boat for the afternoon and had the captain drive us around the coastal Gulf waters for four hours while we wasted shrimp bait, breathed diesel fumes, and didn't catch a damn thing but a headache. This time Dad quietly said something about my wasting money, but I knew what he really meant was, "I didn't fish worth a damn."

Sue Lynn's story has a different ending:

"Going down to the tank with Papa was always a blast. I remember when I was nine years old and I was staying with Papa during a cold holiday and we went fishing down at the tank. We must have stayed out there all day without catching anything. It started to get colder and I was getting tired so we started to reel our lines in. While I was reeling mine in something started to pull my line and it was so strong. When I finally got the line reeled in, at the end of it was this huge catfish! It was the biggest one I had ever caught and Papa was so excited. I still have the picture that Nancy took of me holding that catfish, with Papa standing next to me with this huge grin. That fish was almost twenty inches long."

Patsy has a real funny fish story:

"I remember Pop worrying about his fish at the Henke Place when the drought was at its peak and the water in the tank was almost at the lowest we had ever seen. One Thursday afternoon he and I went to 'rescue' some catfish. Well, after just a bit, it was us that needed rescuing.

It seems that the water was really much deeper than it appeared and the mud in the bottom even deeper than the water. I convinced him that it would be better for me to go into the deeper middle and he stay on the outer edges and that we could dredge or drag a net across and catch the remaining fish that were left. Well, we had lots of fun, cooled off a bit, lost our tennis shoes in the mud and came home with absolutely no fish."

GARDEN

Living on the farm and scratching a living out of the soil made Mom and Dad into super stewards of the earth and its resources. There were times, I'm sure, when we didn't have much money, but we never went without something to eat. We raised all our food except such staples as flour, spices, seasonings, corn meal, coffee, etc. Mom and Rose made all the bread we ate until her later years and canned and preserved everything we grew in the garden. We always had a garden going. She even made some catsup from green mustang grapes. It wasn't very good and she didn't make a second batch, but we did eat the one she made. Her tomato catsup was delicious. I guess my favorite of all the things she put up was her peach preserves. No matter whose peach preserves I eat even now, I think of Mom. Or, were her pickles the best? They sure were good. Oh, how about her canned corn? It was superb. And then, there was her sauerkraut; boy, it was strong. I think she let it ferment about a day too long. Dawn says her green beans were the best. Now, we know she has good taste.

Dad's garden always produced the best of corn, cucumbers, peppers, beans, beets, carrots, radishes, tomatoes, squash, melons, peaches and what ever else you desired. I guess that comes from being 'tuned in' to nature. When you put all these things of the garden together with the chickens, turkeys, beef, and pork we raised and dressed, you can see why they raised a healthy family. Dad even got the idea once after eating and enjoying some mutton barbecue that he should keep a few sheep to provide mutton for our family gatherings. As a result, he kept sheep on the place for many years; not many, but just enough to provide the food we needed. To this day, Dawn recalls that Dad's barbecued mutton was the best barbecue she has ever eaten.

GATHERINGS

If a person was off this planet and looking down upon it to observe what went on at Mom and Dad's house, no doubt the thing that person would find most interesting would be the family gatherings. It is a real mystery how so many people could get together and get along so well together when there was so much diversity within the group. But the thing that would impress that observer from afar the most would be the delight that came over the folks whenever any of the family arrived AND the delight experienced by the visitors.

Gatherings were moments to cherish for years to come and some of those memories are shared here.

Elinor: "We were thrilled when we learned that we were moving to Houston when Lad was assigned to head up the General Electric team to work on the Apollo project with NASA. That was home for eleven years and on our frequent trips to Cuero the children got to know their grandparents, aunts, uncles, and cousins. They also learned to share in the fun, joys, and sorrows of a large family."

Carol: "I remember visiting Grandma and Grandpa and bringing Sandy, our dog. Sandy got off her line and started chasing the chickens. I can still see Grandpa carrying her by her hind legs upside down back into the yard to tie her up. It looked funny, but Grandpa sure didn't think so." AND, "I remember that Grandma couldn't eat tomatoes with seeds. I also remember playing dress-up in Grandma's clothes. What fun that was! AND, "I remember after we moved to Pennsylvania, we drove back to Texas for a gathering and when we arrived in Cuero, we found that Grandma was seriously ill in the hospital."

Nancy: "Every time we would go to visit them, Grandma would be sitting on the swing on the front porch waiting for us. Before we could get out of the car, she was up and saying, 'Get down. Come in.' She was always so happy to see us. Then we would go into the house and almost always there would be the aroma of fresh cookies baking. I have made those same cookies but somehow they just don't taste the same. Grandma always had a jar of her homemade pickles waiting for me. She knew how I loved them. Whenever we had a family meal, my job was to help slice the pickles. I didn't mind one bit because I was able to sneak as many bites as I wanted without getting into trouble.'

Cynthia: "I remember the family gatherings we had at Grandpa and Grandma's house for every kind of occasion. The adults were by themselves and the grandchildren were grouped together by age and gender. I was caught in the middle, too young to hang around with Diana, Peggy, Patricia, Janet, Carol, and Cathy. I thought I was too old to play with Nancy and Becky. Therefore, I remember playing mostly with Chris, riding the tractor and shooting the cows with the BB gun. On one particular occasion, a few of us got the bright idea to clean out the old abandoned Grandma house and play there. We were always told not to mess around that old house, that it could be dangerous. The house was really in bad shape, the porch was falling down and the inside was full of junk. I do remember an old ice box in there and I learned how people lived without a refrigerator. It also had a buggy parked next to the building. Well, we got caught in the house and I was the last one to get out. I was crawling out the front window and saw a large lizard on the wall below. I thought it was one of those chameleons that lived in the desert. It scared the hell out of me so I crawled out real fast and never returned to that house. I also remember filling pitchers of beer to pass around to the adults and sitting in the upstairs bedroom above the porch and watching everybody else."

Cathy: "I remember everyone sitting out on the porch on summer evenings. The adults were drinking beer and visiting while the kids caught lightening bugs. I remember Grandma and Grandpa working hard in their garden every year. I have so many wonderful memories."

That garden was a source of great pride and satisfaction to them since it provided food for the family even when we all moved away. Whenever we returned for a visit, they would always load us up with fresh produce from the garden 'to take a little of the farm home with us.' It never mattered if it was a lot or a little or how far away or how close we lived, taking something home was a way of extending the visit.

Patsy: "When I came into the family, there was only Pop at home. He lived alone after Mom died. I remember when we would have a party at his house, it was always a joke with him that someone had to go to town that particular day at least three times to get items that were forgotten. I guess the funniest item to me was the toothpicks, but THEY HAD TO BE GOTTEN. Everyone loved to come to Pop's house for one of his grand parties. If you listen real close, you can hear the laughter of those parties even to this day. And who can ever forget the feast that followed the day after a gathering; the dinner from all the left-over food was really something to behold."

Elinor again: "Sometime before Dad became real sick, he and I were sitting on the porch. No one else was around. We were talking and he was concerned that some of the grandchildren were not attending church. Somewhere in the conversation, I told Dad he's been a great Patriarch of the family and, in fact, for just about all of Cuero, too. He looked away and had a little smile of satisfaction on his face and a tear in his eye."

Cathy again: "I have many good memories of my aunts, uncles, and cousins and especially of my Grandma and Grandpa in that big old white house."

GETTING HURT

Rose has these stories about injuries when we were kids:

"Mom and Dad always rushed us to the doctor when it was necessary. I remember when Vincent, Ladis, and I were small kids, we were playing in the car in front of the house. I don't know who got the blame, but I was the one with the smashed finger and Dad rushed me to the doctor in Yorktown. I'm sure it taught us not to play in the car again."

And: "We didn't have a bathroom or electric lights when we were small kids at home. We used kerosene lamps for light and two-holers for bathrooms. Two-holers, for those who haven't heard, are outhouses with two holes for two people to potty at a time. One day while on the small holer, something bit me. They found out it must have been a black widow spider so they rushed me to the doctor in Yorktown again. I sure was a sick little girl."

Also, "Late one evening, Dad was talking to the renter by the barn and I was out there, too, playing with one of the renter's kids. We were pulling on a cane stem (or it could have been a stack of cane) and I cut my finger open pretty badly; boy, did I cry!"

Home remedies were used on injuries that didn't warrant a trip to the doctor. Kerosene was the standard disinfectant for cuts and thorns and nail punctures. A slab of bacon was used to draw out any infection from a wound or sore. And every injury, no matter how minor or severe, drew this comment from the rest of the family, "you'll get well before you get married."

GOLDEN WEDDING

The folks enjoyed a good celebration and the best one of all was the party honoring their Golden Wedding Anniversary on August 26, 1974. That was some day to remember.

After enormous preparations that took several days and involved numerous people, the celebration began with a High Mass in which they renewed their marriage vows. This took place in St. Michael Church in Cuero where they worshipped their entire married life. Their attendants were Dad's brother Pete, who had been his best man and Dad's cousin, Anna Warzecha, who had been Mom's maid of honor at their wedding.

Following the Mass, the entire family and each individual family posed for group portraits for posterity. Then we all went to the Yorktown Community Hall in Yorktown for an enormous barbecue dinner and fellowship followed by a dance that evening. It was a celebration like none else and one that no one could forget.

The following write-up appeared in The Cuero Record:

"On Saturday, August 24, Mr. and Mrs. Vincent W. Warzecha of the Mustang Mott Community near Cuero, celebrated their golden wedding anniversary. The celebration began with a concelebrated Mass at St. Michael Church in Cuero with the Right Reverend Monsignor Henry Herbst, pastor, and the Reverend John Flynn, former pastor of St. Michael's, officiating. Assisting at the Mass were the following grandchildren: William Tam of Marrero, Louisiana, N. Michael and Alissa Warzecha of Corpus Christi, Christopher Warzecha of Beaumont, Stephen and Karen Warzecha of Puunene, Hawaii, Peggy Warzecha of Cuero, Sue Lynn Warzecha of Brownsville, and Carol Warzecha of Ormond Beach, Florida. Attendants to Mr. and Mrs. Warzecha were

Pete Warzecha of San Antonio and Anna Warzecha of Yorktown, the best man and maid of honor at the marriage, which took place on August 26, 1924, at Holy Cross Catholic Church in Yorktown. Mr. and Mrs. Warzecha still reside on the farm where they moved after their marriage in 1924.

Following the Mass, the Warzechas were guests of honor at a reception, barbecue supper and dance at the Yorktown Community Hall. Approximately five hundred friends and relatives attended the celebration which was hosted by the Warzechas' seven children: Rose Marie Tam of Yorktown, Vincent J. of Cuero, Ladislaus of Ormond Beach, Florida, Anthony of Beaumont, Newton of Corpus Christi, Robert of Puunene, Hawaii, and David of Brownsville. The Warzechas have twenty-one grandchildren and three great grandchildren.

At the reception, Mr. and Mrs. Warzecha received their well wishers in a receiving line which lasted approximately one hour. Mrs. Warzecha's gown was a long sleeved, full length sheath of gold lace over crepe backed satin with cuffs and bodice embroidered with seed pearls. The grand march at the dance was led by Mr. and Mrs. August Kozielski and it wound around and around the hall for forty minutes. The guest registry reflects visitors from Houston, San Antonio, Victoria, Edna, Corpus Christi, Austin and New Orleans, Louisiana, in addition to the local area."

GOOD FRIENDS

I remember seeing Cecelia Konczewski at Dad's funeral. Mom and Dad had been friends with her and her husband, Walter, for many, many years, exchanging visits in each other's homes and always seeing each other in town, at church, and at social gatherings. Mr. Konczewski and Mom had died before Dad did.

At Dad's funeral, Mrs. Konczewski lamented his death and commented that now her last friend was gone. She had out-lived everyone else and now was going to be lonely. She said that Mom and Dad were such good friends of theirs and she always treasured their friendship. I thanked her for her friendship and for sharing her feelings with our family. Good friends are to be cherished.

HEARING AIDS

Lad recalls:

"As long as I can remember, Mom was hard of hearing. Maybe she got it from some illness or from a stick of wood hitting her in the head when she was cutting firewood to cook dinner on the old wood-burning kitchen stove. Who knows! At some time, she decided to try a hearing aid. The first one was as big as a tobacco can (for those who have never seen a tobacco can, think of two or three cigarette packs) and it hung around her neck. Later, they got small enough that they fit mostly inside and behind the ear. What an inconvenience that must have been! And when she couldn't hear us she wondered what we were whispering so she couldn't hear, all with some justification. In the mid-sixties, she learned that her hearing loss was of a type that might be restored by an operation. She decided to try it in one ear. What a wonderful thing that was. Her hearing in that ear was fully restored. Later, she had the other ear fixed, with equally spectacular results. Hats off to her, Dad and anyone else in the family who might have counseled her and encouraged her to take a shot at it. It made a world of difference in her life."

On that subject, Dawn recalls:

"Mom wore that first instrument tucked away in her brassiere between her breasts and we found it comical how she would adjust the volume during Father Janssen's sermon. We joked with her that she was really turning him off. She compounded the story be neither denying nor confirming what she was up to."

It was good that she had a good sense of humor. Of course, surviving the raising of us seven kids required a sense of humor.

Cathy remembers:

"The thing I remember most about Grandma was her cute little giggle and her sweet disposition. As for Grandpa, I remember him being very sweet and yet, stern. And one thing that stands out most about him was his hearing trouble and his hearing aid."

It's true that he, too, had hearing problems requiring use of a hearing aid, but his hearing loss didn't come until his later years. He was continually having problems with his device as it would whistle real often from an incorrect volume setting. Several of us had, independently of each other, given him amplifiers for the telephone receiver, but he never did seem to get the hang of it or, at least, find them beneficial.

HIPPO

In the summertime when we were picking cotton, the whole family was involved in the project in one form or another. While Dad was hauling one load of cotton to the gin to be processed (that is, the lint separated from the seeds and compressed into a bale), all the boys who were old enough to walk picked the cotton from the stalks in the field along with Mom. Rose had multiple roles. She helped pick when she wasn't fixing meals or caring for the littlest of the boys or washing clothes or caring for the chickens and turkeys. As the oldest of the children, she was expected to carry a big share of the chores. Vince, as the oldest of the boys, was expected to make up for that share of the work that the younger ones couldn't do.

When Dad returned from the gin, he would sometimes bring the cotton seed home for cattle feed during the winter and sometimes he would sell it as a cash crop to have money on hand. Once in a while when he brought the seed home, he'd suggest that we dig around in the mound for our treat. Buried in the bottom of the pile would be a case of Hippo brand Big Red soda water that was ice cold. Boy, <u>that</u> was a treat! Since he didn't do it often, it was a real treat when he did. I don't care how tired we were, that always brightened us up and eased the pain of fatigue.

HOME HAIRCUTS

One of Lad's recollections is about haircuts:

"Dad used to cut the boys' hair when we were kids. It was cheap. It was convenient. And he did a better job than Mr. Jones, the guy in town who charged a quarter (twenty-five cents). Last night while watching the first Presidential debate, I thought about how much better a job both Dad and Mr. Jones did than the guy who cuts Ross Perot's hair."

Another of Lad's recollections is this 'funny' he once came across:

> "M R DUCKS
> M R NOT
> O S A R
> C D E D B D Is
> L I B
> M R DUCKS"

HOUSE

Our house was built in 1936 or 1937. The old house that was there when Mom and Dad married stretched almost East to West with a kitchen including eating area, living room and two bedrooms with a front porch sort of in the middle. Dad had an architect in Cuero draw plans to turn that structure 90 degrees and add on beside it about the same length and to add a second story.

It was a major project and since much of the material was used lumber, it was full of nails. Well, we kids had our work cut out for us. I can't tell you how many blisters our tender hands got pulling old square nails out of lumber that nearly refused to surrender them. It was an important contribution to our new home, though. When finished, it was a magnificent structure and one of the most modern in the community. We did not have an indoor toilet, yet, but there was space for a bathroom and in 1941 Dad had one installed. We also got electricity and a telephone at that time. Until then, we used the outhouse with the Sears Roebuck catalog for wipes, kerosene lamps for light and the old hand pump washing machine and wash board for laundry. Clothes were dried on the lines outside and water was heated in an old wash-pot by the wood pile. It was the same wash-pot Mom used to make lye soap and Dad used to heat water to scald a hog when we butchered.

The house had one bedroom for Mom and Dad, one for Rose, a breakfast room (for every day eating), a kitchen, a dining room, a living room and front, back and side porches down stairs. The second story was a dormitory type open area large enough to sleep at least us six boys, with closets in the attic areas. The upstairs was never painted or decorated because 'who ever goes up there but us?' Naturally, there was no air conditioning except that provided by nature with the windows open. Heating consisted of a small wood stove in Mom and Dad's bedroom and the kitchen stove which was also fueled by wood. As time went by, a kerosene heater was added in the dining room. The only heat upstairs was what we boys generated alternating between arguing and agreeing with each other.

Through Mom and Dad's guidance and direction, this house became a home that was loved by all its occupants.

All seven of us children were born in that house (or its predecessor). Dr. L. W. Novierski from Yorktown delivered the first four of us and Dr. Dobbs from Cuero the last three. I'll never forget the days Bob and David were born, one on September 12, 1937 and the other on September 12, 1941. In each case, Dad raced to the nearest neighbor with a telephone, the Zaiontz family on the Yorktown road, to call Dr. Dobbs to come for the delivery. Vince took all us boys out into the field far from the house to dig up Johnson Grass. By the nature of the activity around the house, we concluded that Mom was having a baby and we hoped real strong that this one would be a girl so Rose would have some help in the kitchen instead of us having to do the dishes, etc. We knew we had to stay in the field until we saw the old doctor drive away. That was our signal that it was okay to come home. We'd race home to find out what it was. You can imagine our disappointment each time when it wasn't a sister. I think after six boys in a row, Mom and Dad gave up, never knowing that the next one would probably be a girl. Hey, as things turned out, we were perfectly happy with the brothers we got. They were fine additions to the family and it would not have been the same without them. God was good to us and He gave us what we needed.

That big house was home for Mom and Dad for all their married life and it served them and their family well. It was the gathering place for the entire family including children, grandchildren, and great grandchildren for occasions of all sorts. Through their love and generous nature they made everyone feel welcome. The true test of someone's hospitality is to have your children's in-laws in your home and get their honest reaction. We can all testify that our in-laws (all of them) had nothing but praise and kind words toward our folks after a stay or visit there.

David and Patsy now have that old house and they are showing it its proper and due respect. Before they moved in, they did some badly needed repairs with a few up-dated twists to give it their personalities. With that house resting in the hands of the youngest of our generation, we feel comfortable that it will have many years of faithful care as it continues to serve the Warzecha family.

JANET'S WEDDING

Carol writes this about Dad's attendance at Janet's wedding. Mom had already died and Dad was living alone on the farm:

"I remember at Janet's wedding when the garter was going to be thrown to all the single guys, Grandpa joined them on the dance floor. (He didn't catch it.)"

Lad recalls:

"We had a great time at Janet's wedding. David and Patsy made it. We wished more of the family could have. But especially I'm glad that Dad was able to make it. He didn't say much, but he had a great time, I know it, and we had a great time together."

Janet and Richard were married in Miami, Florida on May 24, 1986. Dad was not well at the time having struggled in his fight against cancer. He wanted to go to the wedding, but the trip would have been almost too much for him to make alone. David and Patsy were gracious enough and generous enough to arrange their affairs so they could attend and assist Dad with the trip. The rest of us, who could not attend, were and are grateful for them doing so. It was Dad's last vacation trip.

KID LEAVING HOME

With seven kids in the family, there was a constant procession of someone leaving home to start their own lives. Each departure is a story in itself whether it be Rose getting married and moving out or David leaving the nest empty when he headed out on his own. From my own experience as a parent, it's difficult to say if it's harder to turn loose of the first child to go or to the last.

Lad had these thoughts on his leaving:

"In retrospect, I can't help but marvel at the courage Mom and Dad had in encouraging me and letting me go off to college when I was but a few months past sixteen and then, to go off to the Northeast when I was nineteen. They must have known how unprepared I was, and I must have been scared as hell. But they never showed me the doubts they must have felt. That's probably a good thing; I might not have left."

LANGUAGES

Mom spoke, read, and wrote Polish fluently as well as in English. In fact, her prayer book was in the Polish language. When she went to school at Liberty Hill School near Denhawken, the nuns taught all the subjects in Polish, except for English which was taught as a second language. In that way she learned to read and write in both languages. She often communicated with her relatives in Polish. She and they felt more comfortable that way. It was real funny to hear her on the telephone, which was on a party line, talking to one of her relatives or Polish friends because she used English until one of the non-Polish speaking neighbors picked up the phone to listen in on the conversation. She would immediately switch to Polish sending the intruder on her way.

Dad spoke Polish and Spanish in addition to English, but he never learned to write the first two. Spanish was very helpful, almost essential, in communicating with some of the hired hands who did not speak English.

When we were little kids, Polish was the language we spoke at home. In fact, when Rose started school, we converted over to English so she and the rest of us could become proficient in that language. Mom and Dad continued to speak Polish when they didn't want us to understand them. We learned enough of the language to get the drift of the conversation. We often regretted not having learned to use Polish, but our generation looked upon ourselves as "Americans" who should use the national language and customs. Hence, we unwittingly separated ourselves from the Polish culture as it is maintained in some predominately ethnic communities.

From time to time, Mom tried to teach all of us some phrases and we did use a few now and then, but the old saying is true, "Use it or lose it" and we lost it.

Cynthia's memory is good, though, as she recalls:

"I remember Grandma trying to teach me how to speak Polish. It was a short lesson. I think I learned one sentence. Today, when I'm questioned about my ethnic origin, nobody believes I'm Polish with such a short last name. I verify that I'm Polish by speaking the one phrase I know: "Pusta yashe capusta!" which means "Come eat cabbage!"

Hey, if it works, use it.

MEDICAL WONDERS

Some thoughts from Lad on this subject are:

"Never mind the bad tasting medicine that didn't seem to help or those terminal hospital stays that were so heart rending in disappointment. Think of all the successes and what they contributed to our family life.

I don't remember it happening, I guess I was a newborn babe then, but I remember Mom and Dad talking about Dad's appendectomy. It was an emergency affair, seems like the appendix had ruptured. He was lucky to make it to the Yorktown Hospital. He watched that operation with only a local anesthetic of some sort. You can be sure it was not without pain. He was a tough man! But what a wonderful thing for us that he made it."

Newton remembers:

"During the months that Mom was in the hospital just before she died, Dad spent every day with her. Many times I would drive from Corpus Christi to Victoria to see Mom in the late afternoon and then go home with Dad for the night and then back to Victoria with him the next morning. One time when I had gone home with him, I was in bed when I heard this huffing and puffing coming from Mom and Dad's bedroom. I got up to see what was going on. Dad was on the floor doing push-ups. When I asked what he was doing, he said, 'I have to get my exercise.' He was 85 years old at the time."

MEETING THE FOLKS

Elinor recalls:

"My first introduction to Mom and Dad was on the occasion of our wedding in 1954. It never occurred to me that they might not come. Only much later did I realize what a sacrifice it must have been for them to travel such a long distance, on the train, with family and farm responsibilities left to someone else.

My real introduction was our first Christmas at home in Cuero. I particularly remember Mom and Dad getting things ready for Christmas dinner. Everyone congregated in the kitchen. I stood in a corner out of the way and watched. Everyone was talking at once, kidding, cajoling, and telling stories. Mom and Dad were right in the middle and loved it all. And, that's how it was for all their get-togethers."

Carol tells this one:

"I remember when I brought Kevin to Texas to meet Grandpa and the rest of the family. We got out of the car and walked up to the porch steps and Grandpa said to me, 'So you finally hooked one'."

Dawn's meeting the family went like this:

"Tony and I married in Japan and I had never met any of the family. He and I decided that the best way to work things out would be for me to visit my family in California for a while and then come to Texas and wait for him to arrive from Japan and then we'd go to Cuero and I would be able to meet everyone. As it happened, Lillian and Kelly Rodgers were living in San Francisco and somehow I managed to 'hitch' a ride with them to Texas. Besides meeting two wonderful family members, they helped me become a little familiar with 'family' ways and thoughts. They dropped me off in San Antonio where I was to wait for Tony to arrive from Japan. At least, that was the plan Tony and I had worked out. When I telephoned Mom and Dad to let them know I had arrived safely and had found a church for Mass the next morning and was doing fine, etc., Mom announced 'No daughter of mine is going to stay in a hotel in a big city. We will be up there to get you in the morning after Mass and bring you home!' And, that's just what they did. Late the next morning, there was a knock on the door of my room and when I opened it, there stood Dad, Mom, Newton, Bobby, and David all in a row. Dad pointed his head to the luggage, the boys took it and we all trooped down to the old blue Dodge. The boys sat in the back and Dad drove with me sitting between him and Mom. The next two hours were probably the most frightening of my whole life as I really didn't know what to do or say. We arrived at the farm and I began to settle into the routine at the home place.

When I arrived at Mustang Mott, it was only a few weeks until Christmas and all the boys were there. They decided that since I was a 'girl' I would be able to help them get something for Mom's gift. The people in Cuero knew that one of the boys had gotten married, but they were rather confused as to which one, so it was a comedy of errors when I would appear with one or the other in town and the people didn't know exactly to which one I belonged. After Tony arrived home they were really confused. They remembered that he had gotten married in Japan and were amazed that I could speak English so well.

During the period that Lad was home for the holidays that year (1953), he decided that he and I would surprise Mom and fix supper. He wanted to broil some steaks, so he dug out the broiler pan from the stove and was getting everything ready when Mom walked into the kitchen. She looked at the broiler and asked where he found that. He showed her where it was stored under the oven. She was amazed. All the time she had that stove and she never knew the broiler was there.

This was also when David made me feel so good when I arrived at home. He looked me straight in the eye and told me how happy he was that Tony married me. I felt so good! Then he added that now maybe he wouldn't have to do the dishes all the time."

MUSICAL INSTRUMENTS

I'll never forget the year Vince, Lad and I received musical instruments for Christmas. Mom came from a musically inclined family. Grandpa Drzymala and Uncle Fred played the violin and could really make them hum. Uncle Herman played the guitar, Uncle Stanley played both the violin and guitar and Aunt Irene could make the upright piano really sound off. They always took their instruments with them wherever they went, except Aunt Irene, of course. They never missed a chance to perform AND they made fine music together. Mom had a real fine singing voice, a lovely delicate soprano, but she sang only to the small children when she was rocking them to sleep. Once I heard her sing at a school function at Guilford School when I was in the first grade.

Anyway, back to the story of the musical instruments, Mom and Dad (mostly Mom, I suspect) thought the three of us had inherited some musical abilities. And so, one Christmas Vince received an accordion, Lad a guitar and I a violin. What a beautiful thought that was and what an ugly tragedy that turned out to be. None of us could carry a tune in a bucket and we couldn't read music and we had no one to teach us. We were supposed to learn on our own, but no matter how hard we tried, we just couldn't get the hang of it. The only one of us who made any use of the instruments was Lad who used his guitar as a prop when he posed for a snapshot atop old Paint, our riding horse. Lad dressed up in his jeans, boots, and cowboy hat with that guitar in position, a la Gene Autry. I think he used that get up to attract girls' attention.

Lad may still have his guitar and as years have gone by, I think he has figured out how to tune it. He may even know how to strum a chord or two. Vince's accordion and my violin 'bit the dust' a long time ago. I sometimes even have trouble tuning in the radio properly.

Somewhere in the back of my mind must have lurked some feelings of guilt about not being musical because while I was in high school I tried to learn music. I signed up for the band and thought a brass instrument would be right for me. The band director assigned me to the bass horn since all the other positions were taken and there was a desperate need for a bass horn player. When it came time for music instruction, he stationed me and another knucklehead or two in the music room to practice, but provided us with absolutely no guidance or direction or instruction except to practice until we get the hang of it. If you can imagine two or three kids without any musical ability or knowledge trying to figure out how to make horns work, you kind of get the picture. Blowing air through that big horn produced absolutely no sound. One of the other victims discovered that if you pucker up your lips like you're about to kiss some big-lipped girl and then blow into those lips like you were trying to inflate a tire tube, you could create some sound. Boy, it's a wonder they didn't expel us from school for the sounds we made; some were really vulgar.

As I mastered the technique we learned, I discovered how to predict which sound I'd produce whenever I puffed this way or that or held the first, second, or third valve down. Finally, it got to be fun and I looked forward to making more and newer sounds. It's hard to describe them and maybe I shouldn't try. That's right. I shouldn't and I won't. Anyway, in time, the band director figured I had progressed satisfactorily and had me play with the band as they practiced some stirring march. I puffed when I thought I should and fingered those valves as I had learned and produced sounds that thrilled that director. At the end of the song, he publicly praised the fine contribution I was making to the group and said something to the effect that this was the finest bass horn playing he had ever heard. Well, I'm a fool, but not that big a one. I knew right then and there that he knew less about the bass horn than I did and told him my musical career was over.

Ah yes, the Warzecha family was redeemed later when memories faded in the music department and a new band director was on hand and David tried out for band. David had musical ability and he let it flower and bloom as he mastered several instruments: French Horn, Trumpet, Tuba, and Sousaphone. He was good enough for the school to issue him a band uniform and let him play in concerts and at football games.

FINALLY THERE WAS A WARZECHA WHO COULD PLAY A MUSICAL INSTRUMENT.

We're very proud of him for that.

OUTHOUSE AT THE FARM

Lad recalls:

"Everybody had one. Everybody needed one. Everybody used one. Except sometimes not the boys when the night was cold or the moon was dark or the need was urgent. You named it, THE FAMILY OUTHOUSE.

We're talking now of the modern outhouse. Nor necessarily any crescent window cut in the door. But it had a real door and a place to sit. Ours was a two-seater. Or maybe it called a 'two-holer' with one being for adults and the other for juniors. Try as I may, I can't remember being in there with another person, but I clearly remember being yelled at to hurry up and get out of there.

Beyond the seats, or holes, the most universal feature of all farm outhouses was the indispensable SEARS ROEBUCK catalog (last year's issue, of course).

The main use of the catalog was obvious, although they got less useful over time as the advertising industry drove toward use of smoother and slicker paper. But there was a world of liberal education embodied within those catalogs. They presented farm machinery, plows, etc. They showed washing machines and butter churns. They offered motorman's friends for the old timers who had to stay on the job beyond the capabilities of their bladders. And they introduced young boys to the design of young ladies' underclothes that, at that time, they might have spent many years only viewing in their private imaginations.

The outhouse presented a lot of privacy, but it also presented some hazards in daily use. Surely everyone knows the story about the Chinese boys who used George Washington's chopping down the cherry tree as an excuse to deny that they shoved the family toilet (with old dad in the seat) into the Yangtsee River. But there were mundane hazards like black-widow spiders and scorpions. I was lucky. So was everybody else who was never bitten by either. Others were not so lucky. Dad got bit, painfully, a day or so before Newton's wedding. And do I remember right, or was reminded right, that Rose got bit once?

A great institution has passed out of our consciousness for everybody except those lucky few who still live well out in the country. But it's so much better, even at that, than what we've seen in so many other countries. A really great institution!!!

PASTIME

As kids on the farm, we found ways to occupy ourselves whenever there was free time. Sometimes the things we did made sense and sometimes they did not.

I'll never forget how Mom and Dad fussed at us for standing in the ant beds challenging the big red (Harvester) ants. Someone once told us that if you stood barefoot, with your pants rolled up over your knees, in the middle of a bed of big red ants and believed it would work, the ants wouldn't bite you as long as you held your tongue tightly caught between your teeth. Sure enough! The ants would crawl about half way up the calf of the leg and fall off and we'd not get stung. Oh, once in a while one of us got stung, but we attributed that to not biting our tongue properly or momentarily not believing strongly that it would work. Most of the time this happened to our cousins or other kids who had come to visit and ended up testing our story.

Then there were the times we made parachutes out of large bandannas and used kittens to test them.

Or we spit peach seeds out of the upstairs windows while enjoying a snack and ended up with a fine peach tree next to the side porch.

The upstairs windows also provided us with a urinary outlet until Mom caught us relieving ourselves that way. She really got onto us about that.

We also crawled out the upstairs windows to get onto the house roof and scoot around up there like a bunch of monkeys. Dad put a stop to that for fear we'd break some of the wooden shingles.

Sometimes we'd crawl up on the barn roof for a real good view of the surrounding area, but that was more of a thrill than we wanted as that roof was quite steep and slick. It was a faster trip down than we anticipated.

And how about the contests among us boys to see who could urinate over the garage? That was a real challenge and took a strong stream even with a back wind blowing.

Lad has memories of hunting and fishing: "How many kids get to go possum hunting with their dad using a carbide headlamp? Great fun!! Or spend the night on the creek fishing? Or learn to hunt rabbits in the hog pasture? We got to do all those things with Dad and our brothers."

PIONEERS

Lad has some more thoughts:

"The word PIONEERS conjures up images glorified by movies and television. But it fits equally well to some aspects of Mom and Dad's lives that their grandchildren and great-grandchildren would have difficulty visualizing. A partial list of thoughts should include the following;

Their early lives are mostly hearsay to me, but Lindenau had to be sparsely populated when Dad was born at Sandies. Grandpa was an obvious pioneer in settling there, buying large tracts of land there as well as at our home place, at Chicolete and at other locations where others of his family farmed, settled, and raised their families. And only in the later years of his life did modern things like the automobile replace his faithful horses. And Mom's parents started around Kosciusko in late 19th century as well, farming and subsequently in the soda water bottling business in Yorktown before the Depression drove them under and they returned to the roots of farming over a wide area of South Central Texas. Pioneers as well, and Mom and Dad followed as pioneers.

Their early life, growing up on farms and ranches, with Mom's Yorktown city-time sandwiched in, they travelled and courted the old way, by horse and buggy. That's being pioneers!!

For twenty or so years, their home had no electricity, no indoor plumbing, no telephone, no television; none of the many conveniences that we take for granted. These were not hermits or self sacrificing individuals by choice. This was the world they came into and they were determined to succeed and make life better for their family.

Their children, the older ones, started school by riding horseback three or four miles each way, each day, whether it was raining or shining, hot or cold. And occasionally the creek came up and we had to stay at neighbors until Dad rescued us. There was the time Rose broke her arm and still rode a horse to school. And who can forget the thorns in the forehead from those mesquite trees.

I'm sure Mom didn't chop wood because she liked to do it. And Dad didn't spend all day in the fields and pastures for fun. But there were responsibilities to be fulfilled in raising a family and that's just what they had to do.

They got their satisfaction from knowing that they were doing the best they could for their family. They took what talents God had given them and what other gifts He had provided for them and they did the best they could with them. They were very good stewards.

They were very good pioneers.

POP'S TRUCK

Patsy has this recollection about Dad and his last vehicle:

"The day he decided to buy his little truck was something else again. I believe that poor man fretted over that purchase more than anything else. He called several times and even asked what we thought others would say about a man his age buying a new vehicle. But when he actually purchased it and came driving up our driveway at the house in town, he was the proudest man in town. The next day, he loaded that little pickup with so much feed it looked like the original low rider. He drove all over town with that load of feed, too. You could tell how pleased he was!"

PSYCHOLOGY 101

Sometimes I think Mom and Dad were master psychologists, even though Mom had only a 4th grade and Dad only a 7th grade education. They knew how to mold together a group of kids into a family, and one that is still close together after all these years. Each of us is an individual with individual interests and habits, but we all get along together. Even the spouses we have chosen, those who stuck with the family, get along well.

One story I recall about psychology is how Mom and Dad managed to control seven children; at all times whether at home or in church or at school or at a social event or wherever, each child was responsible for the behavior of the next younger in addition to his or her own. That is, Rose was in charge of Vince, Vince in charge of Lad, Lad of me, I of Newton, Newton of Bob and Bob of David. If one of us got into trouble, he got punished as well as the one responsible for him. For example, if I didn't behave, I got punished, but so did Lad for not keeping me out of trouble. It didn't take long for us to figure out how to stay out of trouble and how to negotiate alliances with each other. The system sure did work. I wonder how far people would get with such a program today.

REGRETS

All of us have regrets of varying intensities on varying subjects. Here are some that have been expressed.

Lad:

"There is so much to be joyful about, but there are also some regrets, especially:

> not being around for some more of the good times,
> not being able to help in some of the tougher, trying times,
> not being there to help in times of illness,
> being so far away following our employment needs,
> not having Mom at our children's weddings,
> not saying 'Thank You' and 'I love you' more often."

Gary says:

"I regret that my family never got the chance to meet Grandma and Grandpa, maybe then they would understand the joy of knowing them and the pain of not having them around."

RELIGION

Mom and Dad were staunch Catholics faithful to the teachings of the Church and they saw to it that we got our religious education even though we went to public schools. They both had gone to Catholic schools and had a strong faith. They passed that faith on to us. They saw to it that we studied our lessons and always had Rose or Vince supervise the younger ones studying if they didn't have the time themselves.

For religious education, we attended Saturday afternoon Catechism classes at St. Michael Church in the old wooden two story building that used to be across the street from the Church. Father Janssen and the Sisters didn't give us any slack on our lessons. We were expected to have studied and applied ourselves to our education.

We always went to Sunday Mass together, usually at 10 o'clock which was a sung High Mass. We looked like stair steps wedged between Mom on one end of the pew and Dad at the other. They took their devotion to God seriously and so did we. We are all still active in the Church.

I suspect that they secretly wished that one of us boys had become a priest, but that never happened. The dedication to follow the Will of God that they instilled in all of us DID help me accept God's call to serve Him as a deacon. And so, at the age of 65, I entered into a five year formation program in the Diocese of Victoria for that service and on July 21, 2001, I was ordained a deacon by Bishop David Fellhauer. At the time that I am putting this book together, I have just retired from active ministry. I thank God every day for the guidance and dedication to duty that Mom and Dad exercised in forming me into the person I am. It is with great love that I dedicate this book to their loving memory.

SMILE AND WAVE

Dawn and the boys and I noticed that every time we or anyone else left the folks' house, Mom and Dad would always wait on the porch to smile and wave good-bye. It was as if they were trying to prolong the visit and maintain contact with their guests until the last possible moment as we faded from sight.

We developed our own means of participating in this ritual by alerting each other when the engine was started to 'prepare to smile and wave' and then on signal we would do so. We found that this gesture helped us, too, to extend the visit to its final moment, the moment when we passed out of their sight.

In this regard, Mike has this story;

"I had just bought an old Corvette of '86, and was on my way to Conroe, Texas from Fort Collins, Colorado for a familiarization road trip. The trip initially took me to Austin to visit old friends. Leaving there, the next stop was Cuero. I hoped to have a short visit with Grandpa before moving on, since it had been several years since I had been to 'the place' and seen him.

I stopped at Circle-K, once I got into town, to get something to drink and call ahead. Grandpa was at home and he said he was cooking lunch and would I join him. A few minutes (and many years of memories) later I was at his place. We visited for a few minutes as he finished cooking, then lit into the sausage and potatoes he prepared. Oh, how I enjoyed that sausage! We visited for about an hour, talking about many different things that had happened to each of us in the past few years, good, bad, and just plain interesting.

After a while, Grandpa said he had some things he had to get done and I acknowledged that I had many miles to go that day and should be getting on the road. We then said our good-byes and I got into the car to leave, remembering as I drove off to 'prepare to smile and wave' one last time. That was the last time I saw Grandpa. Grandma was already gone."

SPECIAL MEMORIES

Most of the memories that we all recalled could be slipped into one category or another as I have done, but some could go only into a grouping called "Special Memories." Read them and you'll agree.

Sue Lynn recalls: "The only greatness is unselfish love. Grandma personifies that unselfish love. I only wish she were still alive to share it some more. My memories of growing up in Mustang Mott were of my childhood years, before Grandma passed away. Wonderful things happen when one is around love, but the most wonderful things were seen through my eyes as a child."

Patricia says: "The main memory I have of Grandma and Grandpa is the love they showed to each of us. Delicious homemade oatmeal cookies always in the freezer waiting for any visitor, the fun had on hay rides while the Easter bunny delivered beautiful eggs and candy, rides on the tractor, and the warmth shared with all at the Christmas celebration are just a few of the loving memories I have of Grandma and Grandpa."

Karen: "Because our family lived in Hawaii, coming to Texas and the farm was always a special time. I remember so many small things about Grandma and Grandpa. I remember Grandma always having gum in her purse and getting her hair done on Saturdays. I remember going down to the tank and fishing with Grandpa. Going to Church when the whole Warzecha family was in town was always an event. Grandpa and Grandma seemed so proud when we took up three or four pews in Church. Who could forget the tractor? I remember first only being allowed to ride on it, then as I got older, I was able to drive it. Although the tractor only went 20 MPH (or less), it felt like you were flying down the driveway. The family barbecues were always memorable. There was always so much food. I most especially loved the homemade pickles and being able to find almost any flavor of soda pop in the smokehouse. I also remember the dishes, piles and piles of dishes and all hand washed. One specific memory was Grandpa and Grandma's 50th wedding anniversary. I was asked to participate in the church service which made me feel special. I will never forget Grandpa and Grandma. They were very wonderful and dear people."

Carol said: "The 'something old' that I carried at my wedding was one of Grandma's handkerchiefs."

Nancy: "Grandma and Papa meant many things to me and I have thought about recollections for a long time. It is difficult to put them into words, but I've put down some as I remember them. I vividly remember the evening that Papa surprised everyone with the hand crocheted pillow cases that Grandma made for everyone. No one knew, at the time Grandma made them, but me that she was working on them. I was so thrilled to receive mine. They meant so much to me and they still do. One day I will pass them on to my daughter, Megan."

Vicky recalls: "My memories of summers spent in Cuero with Grandma and Grandpa are pretty fuzzy. All I can really recall are tidbits from here and there without much detail. There is one that has remained in my head about Grandma. I'm not sure when this happened, but it was during dinner one night in the big dining room. I'm not even sure who was present. Grandma was talking and she made a rhyme. It was one of those rhymes that you accidently say, like 'I took off my hat and stepped on the cat.' I wish I could remember the rhyme Grandma said. Anyway, the reason I remember this is because Grandma was so tickled that she made a rhyme, she laughed and said, 'Oh, I made a rhyme.' I'm beginning to think that I was the only one who heard it because every time I tell someone the story, they are clueless. That's the most vivid memory of Grandma that I can recall. I wish there were more. I do have other memories of the farm, like riding that rusty old tractor up and down the driveway too many times to count. I remember playing baseball in front of the house and shooting cans at the tank. Once I shot an old jar of pickles and it blew up everywhere. I remember Sue and I used to walk up and down the driveway looking for pretty rocks and we'd tape them to safety pins and use them for jewelry. I remember sitting outside eating watermelon and the big family gatherings and sweating because it was so much hotter than in Maui. Most of all, I remember having fun!"

Cynthia says: "My last memory of Grandma is the summer before she got sick. Joshua was about eight months old. Mom, Diana, Josh and I had gone to Grandpa to pick the garden. Grandpa was digging potatoes with the tractor. Diana had a couple of seizures so she was in the house resting. That left Mom and me to dig potatoes. Grandma could barely walk good, but she did an excellent job keeping Joshua entertained by pushing him up and down the sidewalk in his stroller. We got all of the potatoes picked and that was probably the last time I had new potatoes from the garden."

Cathy also has a garden story; "After we helped them pick the garden, we would get a soda water from that old refrigerator in the smokehouse. I remember eating watermelon and cantaloupe, ice cold and with salt, on the picnic table late in the afternoon."

Among Sue's memories is this priceless one; "Well, I saved the best for last. For all you folks who are reading this, you probably know what I'm talking about. THE FAMOUS SNIPE HUNT!!! Oh, I was so angry at everyone. What a fool I was. I remember all of us kids getting in the back of the pickup one winter night. There was so much excitement in the air and I just couldn't understand why everyone was excited. Vicky and I were the 'chosen ones' to hold the sacks while all the cousins would 'drive' the snipes into the sacks. You should have heard me calling those snipes! 'Here, snipes, come and get it!' I made kissing noises, owl hoots, even cow noises, but nothing would come. Then I felt something hit the sack and I started screaming and hollering. I was so excited you would have thought I had won the lottery. So, at about mid-night, the elders rounded everybody up and took us back to the house. When we got to the porch, I opened my bag and there was a dead frog in there. Everyone was laughing so hard and I didn't understand why. But little me, I was so determined to 'catch' those snipes. I begged everyone to take me back out to the field so I could catch some more. I still refused to understand that there was no such thing as a snipe. Anyway, when I realized that it was a joke, I was so mad. Not to mention being embarrassed because of all those noises I had made to get those snipes into my bag. All in all, it was one heck of a night to remember. Aunt Barbara sent me a newspaper clipping of a guy on a snipe hunt and it was drawn as a cartoon. It looked just like me! I laughed so hard. By the way, all you cousins that were up at the cattle guard during the hunt, I knew ya'll were there. Ya'll talked and laughed too loud! Gotcha!

By the way, thanks for the memories, wherever you are, Grandma and Grandpa, and the rest of the family. Those were the best of times."

Carol again: "I remember dreaming one morning that Grandpa was floating over my head. I remember saying: 'Grandpa, don't leave me' and waking up crying. A couple of hours later, Mom called to say that Grandpa had died."

Cynthia says: "It seems the cousins really grew up close. I miss those gatherings so much now. I think it is very sad that we have not gathered more since Grandpa's funeral."

STAYING WITH GRANDPA AND GRANDMA

It is said that the love between a child and its grandparents is a special love, one that is without limits and restrictions. That being the case, time spent with grandparents must be a special time in the lives of children.

Here are some thoughts expressed by some of the grandchildren of Mom and Dad.

Nancy: "Sue and I spent many summer vacations with them. We both looked forward to staying with them on the farm. I enjoyed helping Papa outside with all his chores. He was always willing to let me help. I think I enjoyed driving the tractor the most! Grandma was forever baking something for us. She always had sweets in the house for our visits. Grandma enjoyed playing games with us. I think her favorite was the card game called 'Old Maid.' We would go to town with them whenever Grandma had a hair appointment. While she was getting her hair done, we would go with Papa to Stanley's to do the grocery shopping. After all of the errands were run in town, we would inevitably stop at Dairy Queen to get an ice cream cone or a Dilly Bar."

Peggy: "I remember when we lived with Grandma and Grandpa while our house was being built. I used to go to the pen with Grandpa to milk the cow. I would stand on the fence with the cats all around and every once in a while, Grandpa would spray milk on us. It was so unexpected for him to do a thing like that."

And: "Grandma had old dresses and grocery cans that she would let us play with. We dressed up in her clothes and set up store in the hall by their room. She always took the time to cut the bottoms from the cans so they looked full. She kept all kinds of containers just for the store."

And: "I remember her chicken soup. I loved it!"

Also: "I remember when I had a loose tooth that I couldn't pull. Grandma kept offering to 'yank it right out.' She finally convinced me to let her try. She put her arms around me and took the corner of her apron to hold onto the tooth. One big yank and it was out!"

One More: "Of course, there were always the cookies that she made. I would help decorate the Christmas cookies when I was small."

Cathy says: "For a few summers growing up, I remember cleaning that big old house. Janet, Peggy, Diana and I would have that wonderful privilege. It was a big job, but we had the best time. We swept and mopped upstairs and down and we even did windows. One night a week, we would get treated out to eat at the local MOOMOO for some fried chicken or a hamburger. We really did have fun."

And: "I remember Grandma and Grandpa always taking a nap in the afternoon, then eating ice cream around three. I still remember how Grandma would eat hers, slowly taking a little off the spoon at a time, making it last. I remember a lot of Grandma's little sayings, like: 'eat the crust of the bread, it's good for your bust.' (It didn't help me.) And 'don't eat soup when it's too hot, it will crack your teeth.' I also remember Grandpa taking Grandma every week to the beauty shop to get her hair done."

Cynthia: "I remember one time Grandma was staying with Diana, Cathy and me. We were playing Monopoly and Grandma didn't really understand the game and was always running out of money. To help her out, every time she went to the bathroom, we each slipped her some money so we could keep playing and she wouldn't feel so bad."

STORM CELLAR

Lad has these memories of the storm cellar:

"My children, perhaps typical, have probably never heard of the concept of a storm cellar at home, much less imagine that Dad and Mom had one and that we used it a lot when we were kids. I was reminded of it in the summer of 1992 when Janet, Rick, Stephanie, and Kelly were riding out Hurricane Andrew in their home in Miami. Oh, how they could have used the storm cellar at the farm.

The need and concept for the storm cellar was simple. Storms close to the Gulf Coast arose quickly. There were no hurricane radars or search planes and no emergency radio broadcasts. Even radios were rare and there were no TVs or other warning devices. Dark clouds would gather and swirling winds we called 'angry winds' would show us a horrible storm was about to hit. We would grab fresh food and water and our rosaries and get into the cellar. Dad was always the last person in and he would light the kerosene lantern for light and secure the door. Many supplies will have been pre-positioned there for the summer storm season and others will naturally be there on account of the storm cellar's other role as a cool place to store fresh vegetables and home canned foods.

Construction: A hole was dug into the ground about the size of a small room. It was roughly six feet by eight or ten feet and five or six feet deep. The walls and ceiling were wood with the ceiling reinforced by strong heavy beams. This room in the ground was then covered with a layer of dirt mounded up from the surrounding area to provide for adequate drainage. A heavy wooden door slanted upward from the base to the top where it was secured to the cellar ceiling, much like basement doors on some houses up north with external basement entries. The entry way was framed in with lumber and steps carved in the dirt were covered with lumber to provide traction and stability.

Location: It was located close to the house, but not so close that the door might be jammed shut by heavy storm debris. As I recall, it was to the right, or north, of a smokehouse at that time. That put it just about where the present smokehouse stands.

Not every farm house had one of these, but from my earliest recollections, our Dad and Mom had set up this means to protect the family. It was a serious affair and it stayed that way, mostly. I have heard some stories about kids playing 'hide and seek' in there, but I'm sure nobody ever risked 'spin the bottle' with any of Dad's wine from those wonderful grapes from Sandies. You see, the storm cellar doubled as a wine cellar and I doubt if there was a connection, but there might have been one."

On that subject, I recall praying the rosary for deliverance from harm during storms that we rode out within that cellar. Dad recited the lead prayers and Mom led the rest of us with the endings. If one of us started praying without the proper tone or reverence or rhythm, we were reminded that we should always pray as if God were standing behind us watching and listening.

The lessons in prayer that we learned in that cellar in times of fear and apprehension certainly served us well as we found that God does answer all prayers, sometimes in ways that we hadn't expected. Courage to face difficult times and faith that God would and does look after those who acknowledge His being were probably two of the strongest benefits we gained.

I still find great strength and comfort from prayer and I'm sure many others in the family do too.

TO CATCH A CHICKEN THIEF

Here is another of Lad's recollections:

I'm sure we all, the older children anyway, remember this project. At the time of this happening, there was more growth of trees on the home place than in recent years. Trees were thick throughout the pasture that now runs between David's house and Vincent's house. Renter laborers lived in one or more houses in that pasture. There were also lots of trees in the pasture area extending from the barn and watering trough toward the eastern boundary of Newton's place. So, there were several approaches through the woods to the house. That was part of the problem as well as part of the solution.

Dad had noticed that the chicken flock was getting smaller and smaller. He guessed that it must have been one hen at a time that we were losing. There were no signs or sounds of dogs or coyotes getting them. So he and Mom made a plan to catch a chicken thief. Early one morning, we all got into the car with all the stuff we would need to spend the day visiting with Grandpa and Grandma Drzymala at Cheapside, not far from Sandies. The renter laborers probably saw us leave and that was part of the plan. Dad brought his old pistol. Seems to me he took a practice shot the day before to be sure it still worked. Dad drove out of the place and down to where his path back through the woods was well hidden. We drove on without him, but I don't know who drove since we were all too small and Mom never drove OR did she drive this time? My recollection of who drove escapes me at this time. Anyway, we had an unplanned long day visit with Grandpa and Grandma Drzymala.

Dad's plan worked! He got back into the house undetected and took up a good lookout position. Time went on and he kept his watch. It paid off when he caught the thief taking a chicken home for dinner."

Later Lad added this to the story:

"I got to thinking about that old pistol. Maybe somebody in the family still has it or knows a lot more about it than I do. It was a very old fashioned revolver, even then, fifty or so years old. It was probably an old .41 caliber five or six shot model. But the main thing that sticks in my mind was that this was the first and only time I ever saw Dad get that old pistol out of the trunk or wherever he kept it safely hidden away. And I'm pretty sure he test fired it, probably to see if that old ammo still worked. It's not that he didn't have other guns. He had at least one 12 gauge shotgun and one .22 caliber rifle. But, there was something about the danger he faced in this situation that made him feel the need to rely on that old pistol.

Was it the multi-shot capability or the ability to conceal it or the impact on the thief of seeing that thing pointed at him? As I recall, that old gun was very intimidating in itself. Facing the business end of that gun would put the fear of God into the hardest of criminals.

I wonder what ever happened to that pistol."

TRACTOR

Dad took delivery of his tractor on December 26, 1941 and was lucky to get it then because World War II had already begun. Equipment like that was soon frozen for military use and he would not have gotten one until after the war. He bought it from Yorktown Warehouse Co., Inc., the local Ford tractor dealer. It was a Ford Model 9N with lights for night work and cost $845.00. The serial number was 56897 which identified it as a 1941 year model.

In addition to the tractor, Dad bought one plow for $110.00, one cultivator for $141.00, one middle buster for $95.75, a planter for $80.00, and a disc harrow for $146.00. The total purchase price was $1,417.75. He received a $277.75 trade-in allowance for three mules, one horse, a cultivator, a planter and a sulky, leaving a balance of $1,140.00 which he paid in cash according to the Bill of Sale and Receipt for Payment I found in his papers when I was doing the research for this collection of stories.

Prior to getting the tractor, all farming was done with teams of mules and horses. They pulled the plows, cultivators, wagons, hay cutter, planters, and all the other equipment needed for farming.

That tractor was the newest and best piece of equipment a man could own. It ran on gasoline and could be worked day and night thereby increasing the production and capabilities of the farm. It could plow or plant or harvest two rows at a time instead of the single row capacity of the mule drawn equipment and it could travel several times faster. With one son already a teenager and others on the way, it was time to really increase the production of the farm and that tractor made that possible.

He kept a team of mules, Coalie and Julie, for a while for jobs that he didn't think the tractor could handle and for jobs for one boy to do with them while someone else operated the tractor. After a while, he realized the tractor could do everything the mules could do except eat hay so he got rid of them.

That Ford, with its low-slung nature and wide-apart wheels served the farm very well and in later years took many of the grandchildren for rides. It was the source of much delight for the little ones.

TRIPS HOME

Lad recalls some of his trips home:

"Trips home sometimes brought surprises of varied sorts.

There was the time I drove home from Schenectady, New York and made the trip faster than I expected. Suddenly I realized that I would be getting home at three or four in the morning and I didn't want to awaken the folks. It seemed like a good idea to drive to the Henke Place where Vince lived and awaken him. It worked out okay because none of the brothers sleeping there that night remembered where they had left the gun and the dogs and I made a lot of racket when I came in. Maybe I should have gone directly home and slept in the car until morning.

Mom, like all good mothers, worried about us when we were out of sight. She probably worried more about me because I left home so young, was pretty naive anyway, was sentimental, couldn't leave without choking up, and was probably the worst letter writer in the family so that there frequently were weeks without contact. Anyway, one morning while I was home on vacation, Mom needed to go grocery shopping or something and I was anxious to give her a ride in my new car. I had been home a day or two and Vince and I had been out the night before to the White Leghorn or someplace. So Mom and I drove to Cuero and got the shopping done, probably at Piggly-Wiggly. As we were leaving town, we were stopped by a traffic light that I was late in noticing because we were talking or something. I hit the brakes quickly and hard, and we stopped without sliding into the intersection, but not without Vince's pistol and my Jack Daniel's bottle sliding out from under the seat and coming to rest against Mom's feet. What a relief that we were able to laugh about it even though it was a big, bad surprise to both of us."

CHAPTER FOUR

NAMES AND PLACES

NAMES

To clarify and identify who the story tellers are, we offer these brief descriptions:

Rose: First child and only daughter of Vincent and Susie.
Vincent: Or Vince Or Brother—Second child.
Ladislaus: Or Lad Or Ladis—Third child.
Anthony: Or Tony Or I—Fourth child.
Newton: Fifth child.
David: Seventh child.
Barbara: Wife of Vince.
Elinor: Wife of Lad.
Dawn: Wife of Tony.
Patsy: Wife of David.
Cathy: Daughter of Rose and Tony Tam.
Cynthia: Daughter of Rose and Tony Tam.
Peggy: Daughter of Vince and Barbara.
Carol: Daughter of Lad and Elinor.
Gary: Son of Lad and Elinor.

<u>Mike</u>: Son of Tony and Dawn.

<u>Patricia</u>: Daughter of Newton.

<u>Karen</u>: Daughter of Bob and Beverly.

<u>Vicky</u>: Daughter of Bob and Beverly.

<u>Nancy</u>: Daughter of David.

<u>Sue Lynn</u>: Daughter of David.

There is one of the children of Vincent and Susie Warzecha who is not listed as a contributor of stories and that is Robert (Or Bob Or Bobby) who was a very important contributor to the life of this family. Bob died on June 6, 1993 after a courageous but unsuccessful battle with cancer. We all miss him very much and pray that his soul rests in peace with The Lord God.

<u>PLACES</u>

It would be good to know something about the locations mentioned in the story. Well, here we go!

<u>Cuero</u>:

Cuero is the largest town in DeWitt County in Texas and is its County Seat. It is at the intersection of U S highways 183, 77A, and 87. It was organized in 1873 as a half way point between Indianola and San Antonio. It was named for CUERO CREEK which the Spaniards called ARROYO del CUERO, or Creek of the Rawhide. Cuero Creek lies four miles north of the present city. The story handed down from generation to generation is that the local Indians killed wild cattle which were stuck in the mud of the creek and they stretched the hides to dry for use as clothing and shelters and weaponry. The dried cattle hides were called "rawhide", hence, the name Cuero.

Denhawken:

Denhawken is a small rural community fourteen miles east of Floresville in Wilson County. It was established by German and Polish immigrants in the late 1890s. Like many other rural communities, it grew up alongside the railroad that was helping move goods and people into the frontiers that stretched inland.

Indianola:

Indianola was founded in 1846 on Matagorda Bay in Calhoun County. It was developed as a seaport and in its prime was the second busiest and most important seaport in Texas. It became the primary port of entry for immigrants entering Texas from Europe. The town had a population in excess of 5,000 when a disastrous hurricane struck in 1875. With no warning system like we have in modern times, the people were caught off guard resulting in an enormous loss of life and property. The area rebuilt but another hurricane struck on August 20, 1886 and nearly everything was destroyed. Many of the surviving residents and businesses moved to safer ground at Cuero.

Kosciusko:

Twelve miles east of Floresville in Wilson County is the Polish settlement named after the Polish patriot THADDEUS KOSCIUSKO. The Catholic settlers established St. Ann Church in 1892 to serve their needs. The community continues to foster the mixture of the Polish culture with an American flavor.

Lindenau:

Lindenau is on the Farm Road 653 five miles northwest of Cuero in DeWitt County. The original location was near the site of the present St. John Lutheran Church. The town was moved one mile east in 1906 to accommodate the railroad that passed through the area. The Lindenau School remained in the area of the original town site until it closed in the 1970s. In 1942 Guilford School was merged with the Lindenau School. The Warzecha children went to Guilford School and then to Lindenau School at which they received their education up and including the second year of high school. Vincent Warzecha served for many years on the Board of Trustees of both Guilford and Lindenau Schools.

Mustang Mott:

Mustang Mott itself was only a wide spot on the U S highway 87 approximately seven miles west-northwest of Cuero in DeWitt County. All the area surrounding the store at Mustang Mott was considered part of the community. The area got its name from a clump (Mott) of live oak trees nearby which served as a shelter in the "old days" for wild horses called MUSTANGS that inhabited the area. The Warzecha family lived in the Mustang Mott community.

Panna Maria:

Panna Maria is in Karnes County approximately four miles north of Karnes City at the intersection of Farm Roads 81 and 2724. It is the oldest permanent Polish community in America. It is the home of the oldest Catholic Church and school of the Polish tradition. In 1854 the first settlers arrived in time to celebrate Christmas Midnight Mass in a meadow under a large oak tree. They made the area their home and they named it Panna Maria which means Virgin Mary. The 2000 census recorded the community's population at 96 inhabitants.

St. Hedwig:

St. Hedwig is in eastern Bexar County about 16 miles from downtown San Antonio. Farm Roads 1346 and 1518 cross at the heart of the community. It was named for St. Hedwig who was the patron saint of Silesia in Poland since most of the early settlers came from Gross Strehlitz in Upper Silesia. Lately it has blossomed into a rural bedroom community for workers from San Antonio.

Yorktown:

Yorktown came into existence in 1846 when German immigrants settled in the area. It is on State highway 72 in DeWitt County about 75 miles southeast of San Antonio and 17 miles west of Cuero. It served the rural population of farmers and ranchers for many years. In the current time (2012), it is near the center of feverish oil and gas exploration in the Eagle Ford Shale which is producing unimaginable wealth for its landowners.

CHAPTER FIVE

ACKNOWLEDGEMENTS

There is no way that a story such as this one could be told without the cooperation of a lot of people. I am indebted to all the members of the family who offered recollections and memorable stories from their contact and association with the principals of this story. With humble gratitude, I acknowledge their help and the grace of God who has allowed me to prowl through a lot of public records and people's memories for the material I used to focus the spotlight on two of the most beautiful and loving and wonderful people in the world, Vincent and Susie Warzecha, THE WARZECHAS OF MUSTANG MOTT.

CHAPTER SIX

APOLOGIES

This volume is the work of a mortal human being and, as such, is subject to the possibility of errors. Every effort has been made to avoid errors, but some may have simply happened. For any that escaped my detection and correction, I offer my profound apology.

Also, there exists the possibility that some significant information or detail was overlooked. For any such omission, I also apologize.

Finally, for the long delay in completing this project after the initial promises of a quick publication, oh boy, I apologize for that, too.